Simple Foods
for the Pack

No Longer the Property of NOLS

D1206274

North Olympic
Library System
Port Angeles, WA 98362

Sierra Club Outdoor Adventure Guides

Land Navigation Handbook
The Sierra Club Guide to Map and Compass

Walking Softly in the Wilderness
The Sierra Club Guide to Backpacking

Simple Foods for the Pack

Third Edition • Completely Revised

Claudia Axcell

Vikki Kinmont Kath

Diana Cooke

Illustrated by Bob Kinmont

Sierra Club Books

San Francisco

The Sierra Club, founded in 1892 by John Muir, has devoted itself to the study and protection of the earth's scenic and ecological resources—mountains, wetlands, woodlands, wild shores and rivers, deserts and plains. The publishing program of the Sierra Club offers books to the public as a non-profit educational service in the hope that they may enlarge the public's understanding of the Club's basic concerns. The point of view expressed in each book, however, does not necessarily represent that of the Club. The Sierra Club has some sixty chapters throughout the United States and in Canada. For information about how you may participate in its programs to preserve wilderness and the quality of life, please address inquiries to Sierra Club, 85 Second Street, San Francisco, California 94105, or visit our website at www.sierraclub.org.

Text copyright © 2004, 1986, 1976 by Claudia Axcell, Vikki Kinmont Kath, and Diana Cooke

All rights reserved under International and Pan-American Copyright Conventions. No part of this book may be reproduced in any form or by any electronic or mechanical means, including information storage and retrieval systems, without permission in writing from the publisher.

Third Edition

Published by Sierra Club Books
85 Second Street, San Francisco, CA 94105
www.sierraclub.org/books

Produced and distributed by
University of California Press
Berkeley and Los Angeles, California
University of California Press, Ltd.
London, England
www.ucpress.edu

SIERRA CLUB, SIERRA CLUB BOOKS, and the Sierra Club design logos
are registered trademarks of the Sierra Club.

Library of Congress Cataloging-in-Publication Data

Axcell, Claudia, 1946-
    Simple foods for the pack / Claudia Axcell, Vikki Kinmont Kath, and Diana Cooke; illustrated by Bob Kinmont.— 3rd ed.
      p. cm.
    ISBN 1-57805-110-X
    1. Outdoor cookery. 2. Backpacking. 3. Cookery (Natural foods) I. Kath, Vikki Kinmont, 1944- II. Cooke, Diana. III. Title.
TX823.A92 2004
641.5'78—dc22   2003067379

Book and cover design by Lynne O'Neil
Cover photograph © Scott Atkinson
All illustrations © Bob Kinmont, with the exception of the following: page 15 (middle) and page 18 © Claudia Axcell, and page xii © Anna Kinmont

Printed in the United States of America on New Leaf Ecobook 50 acid-free paper, which contains a minimum of 50 percent post-consumer waste, processed chlorine free. Of the balance, 25 percent is Forest Stewardship Council certified to contain no old-growth trees and to be pulped totally chlorine free.

08 07 06 05 04

10 9 8 7 6 5 4 3 2 1

To every seeker along the path

Contents

---

3. Foods to Make in Camp

4. Simple Remedies

"I think," said Christopher Robin,

"that we ought to eat all our provisions now,

so we won't have so much to carry."

—A. A. Milne

Preface

Many things have evolved since the first writing of *Simple Foods for the Pack* almost thirty years ago. We typed the original manuscript on a typewriter, not a computer. Our children played freely in the neighborhoods, and there was no such thing as a "play date." All three meals were cooked and eaten together in the kitchen—and "fast food" places were drive-ins where you ate only if you were on a date or traveling. "Home cooking" was done in the kitchen, not on a show on TV. From those days, we somehow moved into this world of high-tech and fast everything.

However, the unfolding of events in the first few years of this new millennium has caused some of us to consciously slow down our accelerated lifestyle and take stock of what is right in front of us—family, friends, and the refuge of nature. The search for meaning in our lives has brought us back to Mother Earth, and this search makes *Simple Foods* more valuable than ever.

We realize that what hasn't changed is the need for quietude in places of beauty—along streams, high in the mountains, deep in the redwoods, out in the desert, or on a wild beach. It's nourishment for the heart and soul. The need to nourish our bodies while out there hasn't changed, either. This book is about bringing the two together—nourishing our bodies as we seek to nourish our spirits.

Whether you are an extreme hiker, a haiku hiker, or simply seeking to commune with nature, you have a love of the great outdoors. And there's no better way to celebrate this experience than enjoying good food and cooking in the backcountry.

Combining good food with natural surroundings is where this book began and where it is today. Access and availability of healthy food products has greatly expanded in the past thirty years, and this book helped explore that frontier.

When we introduced the concept of prepackaging your own instant soup, as in Spinach Cheese Soup, the only readily available packaged soups on the market listed a long paragraph of mysterious ingredients and gave us heartburn in the backcountry. When we first came out with Peanut Butter Fudge, the only "energy bar" available was the Tiger's Milk Bar. We explained the benefits of drinking herbal teas—and suggested ways to combine them yourself in Herbal Tonic Teas—at a time when herbal combinations were not available in tea bags. Now you can even find herbal teas at truck stops. Nourishing Popped Seeds were, and still are, a novelty. We touted the health wonders of garlic and ginger, and we still do—along with almost every health food magazine on the market today.

In this third, revised edition we have included new recipes that offer tastes from around the world, because the ingredients adapt so well to backpacking and are readily available. We added recipes such as Couscous Pilafs, Burritos, Cilantro Lime Dressing, Thai Crab Cakes, Sun-Dried Tomato Pasta, Quinoa, and All Dal-ed Up Dip (masoor dal from India), to name a few.

We encourage you to try seaweed as a sea vegetable. We suggest toasting it for a snack or trying it in dishes like Wakame Quinoa or Soba Seaweed Salad. We also introduce the dried medicinal Asian mushrooms—shiitake and maitake—so lightweight and so good for you. In Simple Garden for the Pack, we suggest how easy it is to "grow" your own sprouts while hiking. This will add something fresh to your diet after a few days out. And we've thrown in some sumptuous treats as well, such as Skillet Brownies and Chocolate Almond Milk.

We also encourage you to buy organically grown foods whenever and wherever possible. Organic farming practices restore, maintain, and enhance ecological harmony, as well as the humane treatment of animals.

Peruse your local farmers' markets or natural food stores for the many varieties of fresh, in-season fruits and vegetables. Take some home and dry them yourself for your next outdoor adventure.

Finally, we take some time in this edition to celebrate the many young hikers we have enjoyed having by our side over the years. Their early-childhood memories of hiking the trails and sharing meals in camp have stayed with them into adulthood. You can create your own memories by including children in the creation of the menus, the organizing of the pack, the measuring and packaging of the recipes, and the decisions of when to eat what on the trip. In this edition, we have indicated recipes that children would particularly like to make that are also good for them. Having them create their own custom-made Trail Crumbs is a good start. And try out the new family of Sweet-Treat Burritos—Ooey-Gooey Burrito, Cinnamon Tortilla, and Jammy Burrito! With little ones on your trips, there are so many stories to be made and stories to tell.

Now it's up to you. You know where you're going. Get creative. Explore the pages of this book, choose the recipes you like, and make your menus. Check your cupboard, make a shopping list, and go for it. Follow your favorite path. Whatever path you take or foods you decide on, remember to keep it simple and enjoy the nurturing gifts of Mother Earth.

Earth who gave to us this food

Sun who made it ripe and good

Dear earth

Dear sun

Thanks for all you done

—Children's prayer

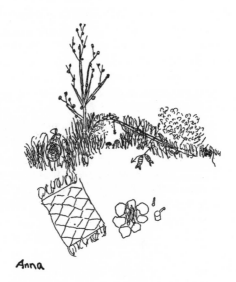

Anna

Acknowledgments

Together we thank Bob Kinmont for his illustrations, and Eva Dienel, our editor.

From Claudia: Thank you to P-nut McCoy, Dick Dorworth, Doug Robinson, and Mike Kaiserski, for guiding me on many adventures through the wilderness. To Annette, my daughter. Thank you for bringing me to the Eastern Sierra and for finding me again. And thank you, Mom, for showing me how to peel my first orange.

From Vikki: I thank Ben, Anna, and Seth—this book is as much a part of your life as mine. Trying out recipes with you on Eastern Sierra trails in the early 1970s when you were children taught me a lot! It's a gift to know that you are now using these recipes with your children as you continue to hike the Sierra. And to Naomi and Tracy for joining in their love and support. To Bob, for first taking me to the "Sierras" and exposing me to their light. To Mike Stutler, for having confidence and for support. To Dann and Donna, for always being there and for the memory of the night our wine froze in our pack at Heart Lake. I thank Pamela Gould, N.D., for expert advice for the Simple Remedies section, and Linn Jensen of the Marin Headlands for sharing her youthful backcountry wisdom. And to the beautiful children in my life— Amanda, Jack, Ian, April, Natasha, Noah, and Jemma—every moment with you is a joy and delight. Thank you for your love and laughter. I am grateful to each of you. May you be blessed with discovery, appreciation, and wonder as you travel your own path.

From Diana: Thank you to Michael, my husband, for his constant support and encouragement.

1

Before You Go

Whether you're adventuring out to places unknown or heading to your favorite spot, getting ready for a trip will fill you with anticipation. Spread out your gear and sift through your backpacking pantry to determine which foods you have on hand. Fill bottles with your favorite spices, bake some Journey Cakes, and test your stove. Mother Nature is waiting.

Planning Your Trip

Playing outside—backpacking, canoeing, climbing—puts a lot of stress on our bodies. We need more protein to replenish strength, more liquids to replace what we use and sweat away, fats to keep us warm, B vitamins to keep nerves and muscles working, and quick-energy foods for fuel. Our appetites get bigger, too, so this edition allows for larger servings. To make backcountry cooking and eating simple, follow these tips:

- Plan your menus in advance, taking into account the season, your destination, how many people are in your party, and how long you'll be away.

- Make a list of ingredients you have on hand and a list of the ones you need to pick up. (For tips on putting together these Basic Foods, see page 7.)

- Check your backpack kitchen equipment (see Tools, page 15) and add any missing items to your list.

- Make sure you have several stuff sacks (in different colors for easy organization), plastic ziplock bags, and small containers for miscellaneous ingredients. (Wide-mouth plastic bottles are good for liquids and staples such as oil, soy sauce, and maple syrup. Plastic roll-up tubes are great for packing peanut butter, honey, and jam.)

- To organize the food in your pack, put all dinners in one stuff sack and breakfasts in another, and plan to keep lunches and snacks within easy reach. Keep staples like garlic, oil, and soy sauce in another stuff sack.

- Make photocopies of the recipes you plan to use and tuck each recipe in the bag with the ingredients.

Caring for the Backcountry

The wilderness is delicate. Please take care and follow these commonsense rules to help preserve the backcountry for future generations.

- Carry and use a stove for cooking. Wood fires are not allowed in many areas.

- Stay on designated trails. Camp at least two hundred feet (seventy adult steps) away from all water sources.

- Do all washing at least two hundred feet away from water sources. If you must use soap, use biodegradable soap sparingly. Carry out all garbage.

- To make a sanitary latrine, walk at least two hundred feet away from all water sources. Dig a cat hole several inches into the dirt. Deposit wastes and bury well. Tamp down. Carry out or burn toilet paper.

Respect and take care of our planet. Leave no trace.

Water

In a wilderness setting, water runs free. It looks so fresh and clean bubbling along in a remote mountain stream, but it could contain an undesirable microscopic bug. While in the backcountry, it's important to choose your drinking-water source carefully and heed the advice of local agencies about the quality of water in your travel area. To prevent the spread of existing pollutants and the introduction of new strains of contaminants to water in the backcountry, it's also important to practice proper sanitation and to educate new backcountry adventurers about these habits. For more information, see Caring for the Backcountry, page 3.

You can do your best to get clean drinking water in the backcountry by educating yourself about the various contaminants and choosing the water-treatment system that is most effective on the contaminants you will encounter and for the type of trip you are planning.

Water contaminants fall into three main categories:

Protozoan cysts. A single-celled parasite ranging from .5 to 15 microns in size, giardia is the most common type of contaminant in this category. Cryptosporidium is another. The most common symptoms—diarrhea, nausea, and stomach cramps—may appear between two and twenty one days after ingestion. Treatment requires prescription drugs; however, these parasites are easily destroyed before ingestion by boiling or filtering water.

Bacteria. Bacteria contamination in water is associated with decaying animals and fish, so look upstream to make sure the source is clear before collecting water. Bacteria can cause nausea, vomiting, and stomach cramps. Boiling, filtering, or chemically treating water will eliminate it.

Viruses. Viruses such as hepatitis A usually reach backcountry water through human waste. Although viruses in the water are uncommon in remote areas, travelers should be cautious when backpacking abroad or in high-use regions. Eliminate them by boiling or chemically treating the water.

Also be aware when traveling through cities and farming communities, where water may be contaminated from agricultural or industrial runoff. To help reduce this risk, boil water, use carbon filters, or carry your own bottled water through these areas.

Water Treatment Methods

In the backcountry, the average adult should drink about four quarts of water per day, but carrying that much water, at about nine pounds per gallon, is impractical. Instead, there are three widely accepted methods of treating water in the backcountry: boiling, chemical treatment, and filtration.

Boiling. Boiling water is 100 percent effective against protozoan cysts, nontoxic bacteria, and viruses. To purify, bring the water to a hard, rolling boil for 1 minute. Disadvantages of this method include carrying extra fuel and drinking water that tastes flat. To help with the flavor, add a pinch of salt or a stalk of dried lemongrass.

Chemical treatment. Chlorine and iodine purifiers are effective against bacteria and viruses, but the hard-shelled protozoan cysts, such as giardia, show strong resistance to these treatments. Many backcountry experts recommend combining chemical treatment with a filter for guaranteed safe water.

Iodine treatments come in tablet, drop, or crystal form. To use, follow dilution instructions carefully. Disadvantages of this treatment method include an unpleasant taste and potential health concerns for some people. Pregnant women and individuals suffering from thyroid conditions should not use iodine.

It's unwise for anyone to use this treatment for an extended length of time.

To treat water using chlorine, add two drops of household bleach, without soap, to a quart of water. This is effective against bacteria and viruses. Used in conjunction with filtration, this system provides an efficient method for obtaining safe water.

Filters and filter-purifiers. Filters can be expensive, but they also provide the taste of pure mountain water that is safe to drink. To effectively trap contaminants, use a filter that has an absolute pore size of one micron or one that has been rated for cyst removal. Filters come in the form of a pump, a squeeze bottle that forces water through a filter as you drink it, or a gravity filter device and container, in which water passes slowly through the filter over a period of several hours. Filters need to be cleaned or changed, but the frequency depends on how often they have been used, the amount of water pumped, and the clarity of your water source. A sign that a filter needs to be changed is when the filter is hard to operate or takes extreme effort to pump.

Self-cleaning filters are good for extended trips when you need to filter a lot of water. A non-self-cleaning filter is your best buy for a short trip. Most filters have replaceable cartridges. Choose clear, still pools for water sources (fast-moving water contains filter-clogging particles).

Another option is a filter-purifier, which combines a filter with a purifying treatment such as iodine resins. Don't use this system if you are pregnant or suffer from a medical condition that requires you to avoid iodine.

Basic Foods

Be prepared to head out to the backcountry anytime. Keep these staples on hand in your home cupboard, and try to buy organic foods whenever and wherever possible.

Berries. Dried, dehydrated, or freeze-dried. Blueberries, strawberries, raspberries, blackberries, elderberries. (See Food Sources, page 268.)

Bouillons and broths. Cubes, powders, pastes. Vegetable, chicken, or mushroom. Look for ones that are low in salt, with no preservatives, MSG, or other additives. (See Food Sources, page 268.)

Bran flakes. Outer coating of whole wheat or oat berries. Good laxative, high in iron.

Bulgur wheat. Cracked wheat that has been parboiled and dried. Needs only to be covered with boiling water and left to soak for 15 to 20 minutes.

Carob powder (or St. John's bread). The ground pod from the honey locust tree. High in potassium, calcium, and phosphorous.

Cheese. Try varieties such as Parmesan, Romano, dry Monterey Jack, aged Gruyère, Gouda, feta, and cheddar. Cheddar is also available in powder form and is good in macaroni and cheese, sprinkled on popcorn, or added to soups.

Chia seeds. Concentrated in protein and food energy, these seeds may be added to almost anything.

Chocolate. A luscious aphrodisiac and stimulant, chocolate lifts our spirits.

Corn. Flour, grits, meal, polenta. All are whole corn, containing the germ, ground to different consistencies. Each type has a different use. See the index. Also see Polenta (page 10).

Couscous. A quick-cooking grainlike pasta made from semolina.

Dried fruits. Dried or freeze-dried. Apricots, peaches, pears, apples, dates, figs, raisins, cherries, currants, prunes, cranberries, pineapple, bananas, mango, papaya. Unsulfured, quick, sweet energy. Rich in minerals. (See Food Sources, page 268.)

Fish and seafood. Fresh, canned, or dried. Clams, shrimp, tuna, bonito, anchovies, fish flakes, trout, iriko, salmon, crab. (See Food Sources, page 268.)

Flaxseed. Untreated, high in phosphorous and niacin. Its mucilaginous quality aids in digestion and has a laxative effect. High in omega-3s.

Garlic. Fresh garlic is lightweight, easy to carry, and takes up little room. We use lots of it and use it freely. Garlic comes in a variety of ways—granules, powder, paste in tubes, chopped in jars. Garlic powder is dried ground garlic, and garlic granules are dried and ground garlic juice. (See Simple Remedies, page 253, for medicinal properties of this wonderful bulb.)

Grains. Unrefined whole grains, flours, and pastas— amaranth, barley, buckwheat, corn, millet, oats, quinoa, rice (wild, brown, basmati, jasmine, short grain, long grain, etc.), rye, wheat. High in B vitamins and protein.

Herbs and spices. Whole or crumbled dried parsley, dill, tarragon, sweet basil, thyme, oregano, chervil, rosemary, bay leaf, sage, savory, herbes de Provence (a classic mix), etc. Allspice, cardamom, cinnamon, cloves, coriander, cumin, curry powder, fennel, fenu-greek, ginger, nutmeg. Little weight, big taste. (See Simple Remedies, page 253, for medicinal uses.)

Honey. Natural, raw. Honey has added food value and is easy to carry in a plastic bottle, and its weight is about the same as that of refined sugar because of its concentrated sweetness. Generally, substitute half as much honey for sugar.

Lentils. A tasty, hearty, quick-cooking legume. From petite French to the largest brown ones, lentils are delicious prepared in so many ways. The fresher the lentils, the quicker they cook. To shorten cooking time, soak lentils about an hour before cooking. Petite French, beluga, and small green take 20 minutes to cook; the larger brown or green take up to 40 minutes. A note on "red lentils" found in natural food stores—these are actually yellow split peas known as masoor dal; they take 20 to 30 minutes to cook.

Maitake mushroom. The recent Western informa-tion about this "medicinal" food long used in Asian medicine indicates that it may help reduce cholesterol and stress, moderate blood sugar, enhance the immune system. (See Food Sources, page 268.)

Milk (cow, goat, or soy) and buttermilk powder. Whole, low-fat, or skim. Used to fortify foods. Adds protein and calcium. For vegans or dairy-intolerant folks, use soy milk powder.

Miso. A salty paste made from fermented soybeans and rice, wheat, or barley. A highly concentrated pro-tein high in antioxidants.

Mushrooms, dried. Shiitake, maitake, Portobello, crimini—there are so many available now. Sliced mushrooms take less time to reconstitute. If you use the whole ones, remove the stems after soaking. (Also see *maitake* and *shiitake*, Home-Dried Mushrooms, page 82, and Food Sources, page 268.)

Noodles and pasta.   Wheat, rice, buckwheat (soba), quinoa, couscous, vegetable, herb, and spice. Quick-cooking, tasty, and the variety is enormous. In the pasta family, angel hair (capellini) cooks in about 3 minutes. Asian noodles are available thick or thin. The thinner the noodle, the quicker it cooks. Some noodles (spring rain, couscous, and fine egg noodles) don't even need cooking; just cover with boiling water. Check out your local grocery store, health food stores, Asian and Italian markets.

Nuts and nut butters.   Almonds, pecans, pine nuts, cashews, Brazil nuts, hazelnuts (filberts), walnuts. Another highly concentrated food rich in protein, calcium, phosphorous, and the "good fats."

Oils.   Vegetable, nut, and seed. Our favorites for the staples stuff sack (page 13) are olive oil and toasted sesame oil.

Pasilla chili.   A mild sweet chili. For a very mild dish, discard the seeds. Available packed in cellophane bags in the Mexican food section of most supermarkets.

Polenta (cornmeal).   Regular or instant. Great base for soups and stews. Cook up a pot of polenta and smother with sauce or soup for a hearty meal.

Quinoa.   A complete protein grain. High in vitamins and minerals. (See Food Sources, page 268.)

Rose hip powder.   The fruit of the rosebush, dried and ground, high in vitamin C. See Beverages and Simple Remedies.

Salt. Kosher and sea salt are our favorites. From fine to coarse grained. Try a salt tasting at home and explore the varieties of this basic element.

Seaweed. This lightweight and adaptable sea vegetable is high in nutrients and minerals. Studies show that it may be helpful to the body in many ways, as an antioxidant, digestive aid, and so much more. There are many sizes, shapes, and tastes to choose from. Here are a few of our favorites: arame, hijiki, nori, kombu, wakame, sea palm. (For more information about seaweed and places to purchase it, see Books & Web Sites, page 272, and Food Sources, page 268.)

Seeds. Pumpkin, sesame, sunflower, squash. Seeds are concentrated protein, high in vitamins and minerals. Use freely.

Sesame seeds. Unhulled, raw. Higher in calcium than milk. A good source of protein, potassium, phosphorus, and vitamins E and F.

Sesame tahini and sesame seed butter. Sesame tahini consists of ground unhulled sesame seeds. Sesame seed butter is ground from hulled sesame seeds. Both are available raw or roasted.

Shiitake mushroom. Studies show that shiitake may help boost immune system reserves and activity. This tasty mushroom has long been used in Asian cooking and in herbal medicines. (See Food Sources, page 268.)

Soy sauce. Tamari, wheat free, low salt. A salty, tasty condiment made from soybeans.

Sweeteners. Maple syrup, honey, molasses, brown rice syrup, date sugar, agave (from the cactus) and beet sugar, various forms of cane sugar—demerara,

Muscovado, Rapadura, turbinado, raw, dark brown, light brown, white.

Tomato paste. Sold in tubes. A little goes a long way.

Tomato powder. Tomato juice that has been sprayed and dried. (See Food Sources, page 268.)

Tomatoes, sun-dried. Sun-dried tomato pieces come dry, packed in olive oil, or in a tube.

Vegetables. Dried, freeze-dried, dehydrated, or flaked. (See Food Sources, page 268.)

Wasabi. Dried horseradish powder.

Wheat germ. The untreated embryo of the wheat berry. High in B and E vitamins.

For more information on nutrient value in foods, see Books & Web Sites, page 272.

Staples for the Stuff Sack

These are the basic ingredients to accompany or add to your home-packaged meals. Carry these staples in a separate stuff sack on every pack trip.

garlic
hard and semi-hard cheeses
herbs and spices
jam in a tube
milk powder
miso
nut butters
olive oil
onion
Parmesan cheese
salt and pepper
soy sauce
sweeteners (honey, maple syrup, and sugars)
toasted sesame oil

emergency bag
    ½ cup rice
    extra meals (one for three days, two for
        five days, etc.)
    herbal teas
    seaweed
    Sesame Animal Crackers (page 53)

A Note on Fresh Foods

A small amount of fresh food is a treat when added to the usual dry diet of backpacking. Here are some fresh foods that keep well and go a long way: cucumbers, potatoes, onions, garlic, cabbage, yams, carrots, oranges, lemons, apples, eggplant, peppers, and beets. (For snow camping, we do not recommend taking fresh food along, except for oranges to eat the first day or so.)

Bring a small grater for carrots, cabbage, apples, and cucumbers, and add them to salads, soups, and stews. Potatoes are good fried for breakfast with onions and garlic or as an accompaniment to a trout dinner. Bake or boil the potatoes at home, cool, and carry them whole in a plastic bag. In camp, chop them into soups, or marinate them with mixed herbs and a dressing for a delicious salad.

Lemons, onions, and garlic have many possibilities, and we recommend taking lots of them along. If you are carrying water, add a sliced whole lemon to a gallon of water to keep it fresh longer.

Chop vegetables at home (use the odds and ends left in the refrigerator) and combine them with cheese and herbs. Put them in a ziplock bag and take them along for a delicious dinner to cook the first night in camp (see Skillet Bake, page 87).

Many of the camp recipes in this book call for dried onion, garlic, or other vegetables. If weight allows, take a fresh onion, garlic, carrot, etc., to substitute for the dried. Check the specific recipe and substitute fresh ingredients to suit your taste. The fresh taste and nutrition will more than make up for the extra weight. Carry fresh foods whole to keep them fresh longer, and chop in camp. For onion recipes that cook for under 5 minutes, sauté the onions first.

Tools

Here are the tools we use for cooking on the trail. We use everything on this list and suggest it as a guideline; however, no two packs are alike.

bowl, medium size, one per person
camp oven (see Stoves, page 16)
camp stove and fuel
can opener
cooking pots, large and small, with lids
cup, drinking and/or measuring
foil
forks, spoons, chopsticks
frying pan
grater
heat diffuser
hot pad
kitchen towel or handkerchief
matches or striker
pancake turner
plastic bags
plastic bottles and containers, assortment
plastic pot scraper
pocketknife with scissors
pot scrubber
rope or cord
safety pins
sharp knife
soap, biodegradable
strainer
string
trivet
whisk
wine or beer opener
wooden stir spoon

Stoves

Stoves are a must for backcountry traveling. Firewood is scarce, and wood fires are banned in many areas. Stoves have a minimal impact on the wilderness and in snow country, and they are a necessity for melting snow into water.

Some important features to look for are type of fuel required, stability on the ground and on snow, stability of pots and skillets on the stove, and ease of operation and performance in cold-weather conditions.

When deciding on the best stove for your backpacking needs, start by choosing a fuel. Some stoves burn only one kind. Others will burn a variety of fuels. Fuels include:

White gas. This has a high heat output, making it a good fuel for quick-cooking or for melting large amounts of snow for water. It can be used for priming and evaporates quickly if spilled. But white gas is very flammable and consumes oxygen rapidly. Be sure your cooking area is well ventilated.

Kerosene. This fuel burns hot but does not ignite easily if spilled. It can be found throughout the world. It does not burn as clean as white gas, however, and it has a noticeable odor.

Propane and butane. These fuels are as convenient and easy to use as turning a knob. They have an immediate maximum heat output and there is no liquid fuel to carry or spill. The fuel must be kept above freezing, however, and disposal of empty butane canisters can be a problem.

You also may want to consider the relative noisiness of various stoves. Pressure-gas stoves are all quieter than those that use liquid fuel. Propane is the best-burning of the pressure gases, in addition to giving more heat per pound than even kerosene. (Gasoline has, surprisingly, less still.) The problem is that propane is packaged in fat, heavy cylinders. However, if you cook enough to use up the pound of fuel inside (enough for several hours), then it becomes more efficient. The cylinders are cheap, and so are the stove heads that burn them. The cylinders can even be refilled from a propane reservoir, such as the 5-gallon canister used for gas grills.

A few accessories to think about taking along are a windscreen, a heat diffuser, a pot blanket (make your own with a folded towel and clothes pin), and camp oven.

To make a simple oven, use a metal cake-ring mold with a heat diffuser. Carry along some heavy-duty foil to use as a lid. The hole in the center of the ring allows the heat to evenly bake the batter or dough.

For more information about stoves and camp ovens, check with your favorite outdoor supply store.

Basic Steaming Directions

After charring many breads, cakes, and puddings over the fierce flame of a backpacking stove, we have developed this method of steaming. It takes 10 to 30 minutes longer this way but is well worth the extra fuel and time: the foods turn out moist with little chance of burning.

You will need two pots, one nesting inside the other. The smaller should be approximately 7 inches in diameter and there should be ½ inch of space or more between it and the larger pot. Tight-fitting lids for both pots are ideal, but aluminum foil and string will also work. To make a lid, crimp foil tightly over the pot and tie it securely with string. Make sure the foil has no holes in it. If your pots are thin, it is a good idea to carry a wire trivet to place between them.

Oil the smaller pot and pour in the batter. Cover with a lid or foil securely tied with string. Place into the larger pot, into which you add enough boiling water to come halfway up the side of the smaller pot. Cover tightly. Keep the water at a steady boil.

Don't peek until the minimum cooking time has elapsed. Use a pot mitt to prevent a steam burn.

Sample Menus

Exercise, high altitude, and fresh air make everyone hungrier. When planning a menu for any trip, remember that you will eat more than you normally do, so prepare to increase the amount of food you will bring. Here are some other tips for easy menu planning:

- Eat the heaviest, most perishable foods first and save the lightest and least perishable foods for the end of the trip.

- To save a lot of guesswork and avoid food shortages, measure portions for each day and each person, then label with the cooking instructions.

- Don't be tempted to dip into the next day's food, and always carry at least two emergency meals.

- Consider having the same no-cook breakfast cereal, such as our hearty Granola (page 35), every morning.

- For lunch, plan to have a grab bag of foods, such as Boston Brown Bread (page 55) or Boiled-Fruit Cake (page 57), made at home, as well as leftovers, assorted cheeses, dried fruits, and nuts.

- You'll have the most time to reflect on the day and hang out in camp at dinner. Consider cooking several small courses, which could be the evening's entertainment.

We all enjoy good food, and cooking for us is the highlight of any trip. Here are some menus we recommend for three-day and five-day excursions.   •

Three-Day Trip

Day One

Dinner

Fresh Vegetable Soup (page 86) sprinkled with
  Popped Seeds (page 83)
Sesame Animal Crackers (page 53) with dry jack
  cheese
Assorted dried fruits
Sunset in the Sierra tea (page 241) with Anzacs
  (page 38)

Day Two

Breakfast

Cold Morning Wheat Cereal (page 100)
Chocolate Almond Milk (page 247) or coffee

Lunch

Potato Cakes (page 61) with mustard and cheddar
  cheese
Sesame Seed Cookies (page 40)
Lemonade (page 245)

Dinner

Cream of Tomato Soup (page 136)
Noodles with Spicy Peanut Sauce (page 157)
Apple Crisp (page 227) or Skillet Brownies
  (page 226)
Passion Plus tea (page 241) or wine

Day Three

Breakfast

Corn Pancakes (page 107) with peanut butter and
  maple syrup
Horchata (page 246)

Lunch

Leftover pancakes or crackers with Citrus Cream
  Cheese Spread (page 78)
Nuts, dried fruit
Tea on the Trail 1 (page 240)

Five-Day Trip

Day One

Dinner

Stuffed Portobello (page 89) with Potato Cakes
(page 61)
Chocolate Poppers (page 41)
Gentle Reflection Tea (page 241) or wine

Day Two

Breakfast

Toasted Oatmeal (page 103) with nuts and dried fruit
Hot "Chocolat" (page 247)

Lunch

Tasty Noodle Soup with Seaweed (page 123)
Rice crackers with Miso Spread (page 76)
Ginger chews
Green tea

Dinner

Thai Crab Cakes (page 211)
Mushroom Rice (page 183)
Cup of Custard (page 231)
Anise Milk Drink (page 248)

Day Three

Breakfast

Buckwheat Pancakes (page 110) with Raisin Sauce
(page 168)
Maté Latte (page 242)

Lunch

Sesame Chia Crackers (page 49) with cheese and
almond or peanut butter
Apricot Date Fudge (page 45)
Sun-Infused Herbal Lemonade (page 243)

Dinner

Lentil Tomato Stew (page 177) with grated cheese
Creamy Tapioca Pudding (page 230)
Ginger Tea (page 244)

Day Four

Breakfast
Quinoa and Fruit Cereal (page 102)
Sunrise in the Sierra tea (page 240)
Lunch
Spinach Cheese Soup (page 133)
Sesame Animal Crackers (page 53) with peanut butter
Skillet Brownies (page 226)
Rose Hip Elixir (page 244)
Dinner
Fish Soup (page 122) with Dilly Dumplings (page
    146) or Spicy Hot and Sour Soup (page 131)
Plain Brown Rice (page 180) with Mushroom Sauce
    (page 163) or Taste of the Forest couscous
    (page 174)
Applesauce (page 225)
Owens River Tea (page 241)

Day Five

Breakfast
Granola (page 35), cold or hot
Chocolate Almond Milk (page 247)
Lunch
Soba Seaweed Salad (page 192)
Crackers and cheese
Nuts and dried fruit
Tea on the Trail 2 (page 240)

Before You Go

Foods to Grab & Go

OK. It's Friday, you're sitting at your desk in your cubbyhole space, and all of a sudden all you can see is the sun glinting off granite and a clear mountain lake. The fragrance of pine is everywhere. You immediately call your best hiking buddy and say, "Let's get outta town tonight!" Plans unfold faster than your high-speed Internet connection; you zip out of the office and dash into your local health food store and grocery store to grab a few things. Uh-oh. What to get?

Welcome to the twenty-first century with its multitude of healthy products. Although we recommend that you take the time to put your meals together yourself, the next best thing is to take advantage of ready-made products that are healthy.

In the store, while you are roaming the aisles, think lightweight and high energy. And don't forget the stuff in the fridge. Cook it up (sauté, steam) and throw it in doubled ziplock plastic bags to warm up in camp, adding cheese, nuts, and whatever else you'd like. Also, check your pantry for Basic Foods (page 7) and fill your Staples for the Stuff Sack bag (see page 13).

If you find yourself making last-minute backpacking trips often, you may want to order bulk products online and keep them in your pantry. (See the list of Food Sources on page 268.)

Here are some ideas for ready-to-go foods that are good for you.

Snacks
chocolate bars
dried fruit
energy bars
ginger chews or crystallized ginger
honey sticks
licorice

nuts (salted roasted peanuts, mixed nuts, pistachios),
    seeds
seaweed snacks—chips, bars, pieces to toast in camp
trail mixes

Breakfasts & Lunches
bagels
dense, thinly sliced bread
dense crackers
dry or semidry cheese
granola
honey
nut butters
pancake mix
smoked salmon

Dinners
grains—rice, quinoa, etc., to eat plain
instant packaged soups and ramen from health
    food stores
packaged grain meals
packaged instant sauces
pastas and packaged pasta sauces
tubes of sauces (pesto, anchovy, tomato, etc.)

Desserts
instant rice pudding packages (need vanilla)
lightweight cookies

Drinks
chai
coffee
herbal teas
hot chocolate packets
yerba maté

Two monks, one older than the other, were traveling in a remote mountain region, visiting from temple to temple. They had heard of a great master living in a temple high up on the mountain and started out on the trail to visit him. Just as they were turning up toward the temple, a lettuce leaf came floating down the creek. The young monk exclaimed at the waste and questioned the greatness of the master. Just as he did so, the tenzo (head cook) came running down over boulders and grass with beard and robes flying, pursuing the lost lettuce leaf.

2

Foods to Make at Home

Imagine pulling out homemade ready-to-eat food on the trail or in camp at the end of a long day of hiking. You know what comforts and nourishes you—you made it at home because it's what you like to eat! All the preparing you did ahead of time is now paying off as you relish the accomplishments of your grand adventure. An aroma and flavor of home while surrounded by the peacefulness of nature . . . what a gift this life is!

Pocket Foods

Keep these snacks within easy reach for an energy boost whenever needed—on the trail, on a ski tour, floating down a river, sitting on a ledge or up in a tree, in the tent at night, in the rain, or anytime you're hungry. Prepare your favorites at home for quick, easy, healthy treats.

Home-Dried Apples

Gravensteins, pippins, golden delicious, or Macintosh—check out your local farmers' market for the many heirloom varieties that are now available.

Wash the apples well. If they have been waxed, use castile soap. Remove the core and slice the apples in rings ⅛–¼ inch thick. Thread a string through the center of each of the rings. Then hang the string horizontally, like a clothesline, in a warm, dry area. Be sure the rings don't touch. Let hang for several days.

Trail Crumbs

These mixtures of dried fruits, nuts, and seeds are great for munching anytime. Following are our favorite combinations, but don't feel limited.

almonds, Brazil nuts, raisins, soy nuts, dates, and
    carob chips
sunflower seeds and raisins
cashews, raisins, raw peanuts, sunflower seeds, and
    rose hips
almonds and apricots
salted soy nuts and raisins
walnuts, dates, coconut chunks, sunflower seeds, and
    carob chips
pecans and currants
pumpkin seeds and figs

Fruit Leather

This is a dried-fruit sweet treat. Break off pieces to suck on while you're hiking—they melt in your mouth and are a good replacement for hard candy. When you have an excess of fresh ripe fruit or berries, plan ahead and dry some in thin shallow "peels" in the sun. The fruit dries quickly and easily.

apricots
peaches
plums
any berries
apple *or* pear sauce
almond extract, honey, *or*
      lemon juice (optional)

Wash and dry the ripe fruit. Place the whole fruit or apple or pear sauce in a ricer and press through into a bowl, discarding the skins or seeds left in the ricer. Add to taste almond extract, honey, or lemon juice. Mix well.

Pour the fruit sauce in a puddle in the middle of a glass cake or pie pan and spread to ¼ inch thick and to within ½ inch of all edges.

Place the pan in the sun for a day, bringing it in as the sun goes down in order to avoid dew. Cover for the evening with an open paper bag or cheesecloth to keep the fruit clean. Return to the sun the following day and repeat until dry. In summer, the process should take 3–4 days. When finished, peel the leather off the pan, lay it on a piece of waxed paper or plastic wrap, and roll it up. Seal the leather in a plastic bag and store it in a cool, dry, dark place.

If a storm comes up for the day, put the pan in the oven at the lowest heat possible and leave the door slightly open. Watch the sauce carefully. When it is dry enough to be lifted off the pan, place it on oven racks so both sides dry.

Toasted Nuts/Moroccan Nuts

Nuts, which supply fats and proteins that are so valuable when hiking, can add great dimension to backpacking menus. Simply toasted in a frying pan at the campsite before you start cooking, they can be eaten as an appetizer or as an accompaniment to any meal. The aroma of them toasting in camp creates an atmosphere of harmony and immediately satisfies the deepest hunger pangs. Prepared with spices at home before you go, they are wonderful trail food, and the toasted aroma fills the air whenever you open the bag.

The simplest way to toast nuts is to heat a heavy-bottomed frying pan over high heat, reduce heat to medium, put the nuts in, and stir continuously until they brown, about 5–10 minutes. Or you can put them on a cookie sheet in a 250°F oven and stir them occasionally, until toasted, about 15–20 minutes.

Here's a recipe to make at home that will definitely spice up your day and create that extra stamina and endurance needed to keep on truckin'.

¼ cup vegetable *or* olive oil
1 teaspoon ground cumin
1 teaspoon ground cayenne
1 tablespoon sugar
¾ teaspoon salt
3 cups nuts (walnuts, pecans, filberts, etc.)

In a frying pan over medium heat, stir in oil, cumin, and cayenne. Slowly add in the sugar and salt and continue to stir—about 1 minute. Add the nuts and stir briefly and quickly, just enough to coat them with the spiced oil. Spread them loosely on a cookie sheet and bake at 250–300°F for 20 minutes or until toasted. Cool and pack in an airtight bag.

Spicy Seed Snack

makes approximately 2 cups

These quantities may be varied according to taste.

1 cup pumpkin seeds
1 cup sunflower seeds
2 tablespoons toasted sesame oil
1 tablespoon tamari
1 teaspoon curry powder
½ teaspoon cayenne
⅛ teaspoon garlic granules (optional)

Combine all ingredients thoroughly. Sprinkle into a shallow baking pan. Bake in a 350°F oven for 20–25 minutes, stirring occasionally. Store in an airtight container when cool.

Toasted Seaweed

Seaweed as a sea vegetable is finally reaching the North American market—and our taste buds. For backpackers, it is a lightweight, healthy, and tasty snack. It can also be cooked and added to a variety of menus. (For more information about the health benefits of seaweed, see Basic Foods, page 7.)

Start by picking up a pack of toasted sea palms and nibble on those. Combine these toasted crunchies in your Trail Crumb bags or simply carry little packets of them in your pocket to munch every now and then. Crumble them up and sprinkle them on soups and grains or add to your pots of beans. Toasted dulse is best ground up when used in cooking or sprinkled on food instead of salt.

It's easy to toast your own. At home, fire up the cast-iron pan over medium heat and get it good and hot. Add a small amount of seaweed (kombu, dulse, sea palm, wakame, or nori) and stir continually for 30 seconds to 1 minute. Seaweed tends to burn quickly, so watch it carefully. You may also toast it in the oven. Put various sea vegetables on an ungreased cookie sheet in a 350°F oven, checking and turning every minute, for up to 3 minutes.

Fruit Pemmican

makes 1 8-inch-square pan's worth

These chewy fruit-nut bars are high in protein and good for eating on the trail or in your tent when it's pocket-food weather.

1 cup raisins
¼ cup honey
½ cup milk powder
½ cup raw wheat germ
⅓ cup soy flour
¼ cup wheat bran
½ cup each almonds, walnuts, Brazil nuts *or* filberts, whole or chopped
2 tablespoons canola oil
enough grape *or* apple juice to make a thick batter

Mix all ingredients well. Spread into a greased 8-inch square pan. Bake in a 300°F oven for 30–40 minutes or until firm. Cut into squares but allow to cool before removing from pan. Wrap individually.

Variation: Add ¼ cup dates or chopped apricots.

Granola

==

makes approximately 1 gallon

Serve this granola with stewed fruit, hot or cold milk, water, mint or rose hip tea, or just plain dry as a pocket food.

½ cup canola oil
½ cup honey
½ cup sorghum, molasses, *or* maple syrup
1 tablespoon vanilla
¼ cup milk powder
2 tablespoons nutritional yeast
1 tablespoon grated orange *or* lemon peel
1 cup raw wheat germ
5 cups rolled oats
2 cups rolled wheat
2 cups rolled rye
1 cup unsweetened coconut
2 cups raisins *or* currants
1 cup each cashews, almonds, pitted dates, sunflower
      seeds

Warm oil, honey, and syrup in a large pot over low heat until thin. Remove from heat. Add remaining ingredients in the order given, except the fruit, nuts, and seeds. Stir well after each addition. Spread mixture onto two large ungreased cookie sheets with sides. Bake at 250°F for 1½–2 hours, stirring occasionally. Cool. Stir in remaining ingredients. Store in an airtight container.

For the trail, package in individual meal-size portions.

To serve warm, add milk powder and hot water.

Variation: Toast nuts and seeds on a cookie sheet in the oven at 325°F for 10 minutes, then add to granola with the dried fruit.

Granola Bars

makes 2 8-inch-square pans' worth

These are chewy, sweet, filling, satisfying, easy to pack, and good when your energy is low.

Follow the Granola recipe (page 35), using 6 cups of rolled grains instead of 9. Press raw mixture into two 8-inch square pans and bake at 300°F for 30–40 minutes or until golden brown. Cut while hot, but cool before removing from pan. May be wrapped individually.

Raw Granola (Muesli)

makes 5 cups

Serve as is with milk, fruit juice, or hot tea. Or, for a hot cereal, stir in boiling water.

1 cup rolled oats, chopped fine
1 cup rolled wheat, chopped fine
½ cup almonds, chopped small
½ cup filberts, chopped small
½ cup raw wheat germ
½ cup unsweetened coconut
½ cup dried apples, chopped small
½ cup raisins
2 tablespoons bran flakes
2 tablespoons dry grated lemon peel
1 tablespoon rose hip powder (optional)

Combine all ingredients. Store in a covered jar. For convenience, package in individual meal-size portions.

Cheese Cookies

━━━━━━━━━━━━━━━━━━━━━━━━━━━━

makes approximately 2 dozen

Try these crackers and cheese rolled into one delicious high-protein snack.

½ pound medium cheddar cheese, grated
1 cup whole wheat flour
3 tablespoons olive oil
¼ teaspoon salt
dash of cayenne
3–4 tablespoons milk
⅓ cup finely chopped pecans *or* walnuts (*or* save
     whole to put on top)

Mix grated cheese, flour, oil, salt, and cayenne until they have an even, crumbly texture. Add milk and chopped nuts and knead into a large ball. Form balls about 1 inch in diameter and mash them between your palms. Place on an oiled cookie sheet. If you didn't add nuts to the mixture, place a half nut meat into the center top of each cookie. Bake at 350°F for 20 minutes.

Anzacs

makes approximately 2 dozen

This is an Australian recipe from World War I, when Australian women baked these biscuits (cookies) to send to their men on the beaches of Gallipoli. They were still fresh after an 8-week boat trip! *Anzac* stands for Australian–New Zealand Army Corps.

1 cup whole wheat flour
1 cup unsweetened coconut
1 cup brown sugar
1 cup rolled oats
½ cup butter
2 tablespoons water
½ teaspoon baking soda
1 tablespoon golden syrup, molasses, *or* honey

Combine flour, coconut, sugar, and oats in a large bowl. Mix well. In a small saucepan melt butter with water, baking soda, and syrup. Add to the dry ingredients, and mix well with your hands. Shape into 2-inch-diameter cookies and bake on an oiled cookie sheet at 350°F for about 20 minutes or until nice and brown. Cool on a rack.

38   *Pocket Foods*

High-Protein Almond Cookies

makes approximately 3 dozen

Mmmmmmmm. Serve with chai, coffee, or tea.

2¼ cups whole wheat flour
1 cup almond meal
¾ cup oat flour
½ cup chopped pecans
¼ cup soy flour
¼–½ cup currants *or* raisins
2 tablespoons chia seeds
1 teaspoon coriander
½ teaspoon salt
½ cup apple juice *or* water
½ cup honey
¼ cup canola oil
1 teaspoon almond extract

Mix all dry ingredients in one bowl and liquid ingredients in another. Combine the two and blend well. Form into 1-inch balls, place on an ungreased cookie sheet, and press down with a fork. Bake at 350°F for 15–20 minutes.

Sesame Seed Cookies

These are crunchy, satisfying, and high in protein.

1 cup sesame seeds
½ cup unsweetened coconut
2 eggs
½ cup canola oil *or* butter
½ cup honey
1 teaspoon vanilla
2¼ cups whole wheat flour
½ teaspoon salt

In a skillet over moderate heat, toast sesame seeds and coconut until they are light brown; stir frequently. Combine the eggs, oil, honey, and vanilla, and stir in the toasted seeds and coconut. Blend in the flour and salt, and stir well. Form into balls about 1 inch in diameter, place on an ungreased cookie sheet, and press down with a fork. Bake at 325°F for 15 minutes.

Chocolate Poppers

makes approximately 2 dozen

These treats are great for chocolate lovers.

½ cup almond butter
1 teaspoon vanilla
3 tablespoons high-quality cocoa
3 tablespoons organic evaporated cane juice
2 tablespoons chocolate chips

Combine almond butter and vanilla and mix well. Add remaining ingredients, kneading well with a wooden spoon. Form into 1-inch balls.

Variations: Roll balls in any of the following: cocoa, nut meal, shredded unsweetened coconut. Add 1 tablespoon currants or raisins or 1 teaspoon Amaretto or your favorite liqueur.

Peanut Butter Fudge

makes approximately 1 pound

This is the original energy bar!

1 cup crunchy peanut butter
½ cup soy milk powder *or* regular milk powder
½ cup raisins
¼ cup sesame seeds
⅛ cup raw wheat germ
⅛–½ cup honey

Mix all ingredients until thoroughly blended. Carry in a lidded plastic container and break off pieces as you wish.

Cashew Fudge

makes approximately ¾ pound

This sweet and mild candy is high in protein.

½ cup cashew butter
½ cup chopped cashews
¼ cup currants *or* chopped raisins
¼ cup soy milk powder *or* ½ cup wheat germ flakes
2 tablespoons honey

Mix all ingredients until thoroughly blended. Carry in a lidded plastic container.

Pecan Fudge

makes approximately 1¾ pounds

This candy is like an energy bar, high in protein and calories. It's a good snack to have within easy reach along the trail.

½ cup honey
½ cup peanut butter
½ cup rolled oats
½ cup unsweetened coconut
½ cup chopped pecans
2 tablespoons soy flour
1 tablespoon raw wheat germ
handful of peanuts, sunflower seeds, and sesame
      seeds (chopped or ground)
2 teaspoons vanilla
1 teaspoon lemon juice

Mix ingredients in the order listed and knead a little. Carry in a lidded plastic container.

Sesame Butter Fudge

makes approximately 1 pound

This candy is high in calcium, with a taste and texture similar to halvah.

1 cup sesame butter
½ cup almonds, ground fine
¼ cup honey
handful of currants *or* raisins

Combine all ingredients and knead well. Carry in a lidded plastic container.

Sesame Almond Fudge

makes approximately 1 pound

This fudge is a good source of calcium. For added nutrition, form into balls and roll in shredded coconut.

1 cup sesame seeds
½ cup almonds
½ cup cashew butter *or* peanut butter
¼ cup currants *or* chopped raisins
2 tablespoons honey
1 tablespoon or more water as needed to hold
    mixture together

Grind sesame seeds and almonds. Add the rest of the ingredients, mix well, and pack in a lidded plastic container.

Carob Fudge

makes approximately ½ pound

Sesame or sunflower seeds add good nutrition to this yummy carob treat.

1 cup sesame *or* sunflower seeds
2 tablespoons carob powder
2 tablespoons honey (optional)
1 tablespoon water

Grind the seeds, and mix all ingredients well in a bowl. Pack in a lidded plastic container.

Variations: Add ¼ cup coconut or ½ cup currants or chopped raisins.

Seed Date Fudge

makes approximately 1¼ pounds

Seeds are so good for us, and mixed with dates they are a treat for the sweet tooth.

½ cup sesame seeds
½ cup sunflower seeds
1 tablespoon flaxseeds
1 cup chopped dates
½ cup sesame butter
2 tablespoons chia seeds
¼ cup maple syrup (optional)

Grind sesame, sunflower, and flaxseeds. Combine them with remaining ingredients, and mix well with your hands. Carry in a lidded plastic container.

Apricot Date Fudge

makes approximately 1½ pounds

This fudge is a sweet blend of scrumptious fruits.

1 cup apricots
1 cup dates
handful of raisins *or* currants
1 cup walnuts *or* pecans
2 tablespoons raw wheat germ
1 cup coconut, unsweetened macaroon
juice from ½ lime *or* lemon

Grind the fruit, nuts, and wheat germ in a hand-cranked food grinder. Knead in the coconut and lime juice until everything is mixed well. Carry in a lidded plastic container.

Cinnamon Orange Liquor Fudge

makes approximately 2 cups (20–30 balls)

This is definitely adult fare! It keeps very well, and if by chance you can manage to hide some, it is great even a couple of weeks later.

2 cups graham cracker crumbs
⅓ cup Grand Marnier *or* light rum
2 tablespoons cocoa powder
2 teaspoons cinnamon
1 teaspoon powdered orange peel *or* 2 teaspoons
    freshly grated orange rind
1 cup sifted powdered sugar
¼ cup butter, melted

If you buy graham crackers in a box, they usually come with three packets inside. Crush an unopened packet until the crackers are crumbs. One packet equals 1½ cups, and you will need to crush three more crackers to equal 2 cups.

Combine everything in a bowl and squeeze between your fingers until the mixture forms a ball. May be packed in one large ball or divided into small balls and rolled in a combination of powdered sugar and cocoa powder.

The fudge will harden if not kept sealed in an airtight bag. Keep it away from the sun as you would a chocolate bar.

Sesame Crisp Candy

makes 1 9-by-13-inch pan's worth

This tasty treat is crispy, crunchy, chewy, and sweet.

2 cups sesame seeds
½ cup almonds, walnuts, pecans, *or* hazelnuts,
    chopped
½ cup honey
½ cup brown sugar
1 teaspoon ginger
1 teaspoon cinnamon
4 cardamom pods, husks removed

In a moderate oven (350°F), toast the sesame seeds and nuts for 15 minutes. Meanwhile, in a frying pan over medium heat, melt the honey, sugar, and spices. Stirring constantly, bring to a boil and cook 2 minutes. Remove from heat and stir in seeds and nuts, mixing well. Turn into an oiled 9-by-13-inch pan and press flat. Cut while slightly warm. Cool before wrapping.

Variations: Add ½ cup chopped dried dates or cranberries, or ½ cup coconut.

Breads & Crackers

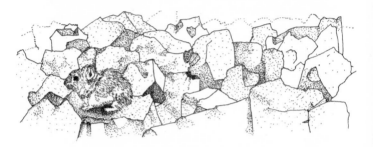

Here are a few bread and cracker recipes to make ahead that are particularly high in protein and extra nourishment. For additional bread recipes, see Breads to Make in Camp, page 111.

Zwieback

Got a drooling baby in your pack? Take along zwieback.

This is a good idea for any whole-grain yeasted bread. It makes the bread lightweight and long lasting. Zwieback may be broken into soups or salads to add crunchiness.

Slice bread ½ inch thick or a little thicker and bake on open oven racks at 225°F for approximately 2½ hours. Carry in a plastic bag.

Sesame Chia Crackers

makes approximately 2 dozen

These crunchy crackers are easy to make.

2 cups whole wheat flour *or* 1½ cups oat flour plus ¾
     cup soy flour
½ cup sesame seeds
2 tablespoons chia seeds
1 teaspoon salt
⅓ cup sesame oil
½ cup water

In a bowl, mix flour, sesame and chia seeds, and salt. Stir in oil and mix to an even consistency. Add water and shape dough into a large ball. Sprinkle extra sesame seeds on waxed paper and roll dough on paper to about ¼ inch thick. Cut into cracker shapes. Remove crackers from waxed paper, place on an ungreased cookie sheet, and bake at 375°F for 15–20 minutes. Cool before packaging.

High-Protein Crackers

makes approximately 2 dozen

Serve these with lunch or dinner. They take the place of bread and are tasty and crunchy.

1 cup whole wheat flour
1 cup rye flour
½ cup soy flour
½ cup raw wheat germ
½ cup sesame seeds
1 tablespoon chia seeds (optional)
⅓ cup olive *or* walnut oil
enough cold water to make a stiff dough
1 teaspoon coarse-ground sea salt

In a bowl, combine dry ingredients except salt, and mix well. Stir in the oil and mix to an even consistency. Add water to make a stiff dough. Knead 10–20 times and let stand a few minutes. On a floured surface, roll the dough very thin, sprinkle on salt and a few extra sesame seeds, and roll again, pushing the salt and seeds well into the dough. Make holes with a fork, and then cut dough into desired shapes. Bake on an ungreased cookie sheet at 300°F until golden brown and crisp, about 15–20 minutes. Cool before packaging.

Corn Crackers

===================================

Try these yummy crackers with Cream of Tomato Soup (page 136).

2 cups whole wheat flour
1 cup cornmeal
½ cup sesame seeds
pinch of salt
¼ cup olive oil
2 tablespoons honey
1 cup water, or more

Combine dry ingredients. In a separate bowl, mix together oil, honey, and water and add to dry ingredients. Mix well with your hands, adding extra water if necessary. On a floured surface, roll dough to about ¼ inch thick. Cut into cracker shapes and bake on an oiled cookie sheet at 350°F for 20 minutes or until crisp and lightly browned. Cool before packaging.

Graham Crackers

▬▬▬▬▬▬▬▬▬▬▬▬▬▬▬▬▬▬▬▬▬▬▬▬▬

makes 4–5 dozen

These are far removed from store-bought graham crackers. They're less fragile and very filling.

¾ cup butter
½ cup honey
1 teaspoon vanilla
3 cups graham *or* whole wheat flour
½ cup raw wheat germ
1 teaspoon cinnamon
½ teaspoon baking powder
¾ cup water

Beat butter, honey, and vanilla until fluffy. Combine dry ingredients and add alternately with the water to the creamed mixture. Roll out on a floured surface to about ¼ inch thick, cut into squares, and place on an ungreased cookie sheet. Prick each cracker a couple of times with a fork. Bake at 325° for 20–25 minutes or until nicely browned. Cool on a rack before packaging.

Sesame Animal Crackers

makes approximately 6 dozen

Kids will love these tasty, crunchy crackers. Use your favorite cookie cutters to make fun shapes. The lions and tigers and bears are yummy spread with peanut butter or dipped in honey. Try them with dry jack cheese, too.

1 cup wheat flour
1 cup sesame seeds
1½ cups instant *or* quick rolled oats
½ cup rice flour
½ cup coconut
1½ teaspoons salt
¼ cup sugar
¼ cup canola oil
½ cup water

Combine dry ingredients and mix well. Add oil and water and mix well again. Let stand 5–10 minutes. If dough is dry and falls apart, add a little more water. Divide into quarters. On a lightly floured surface, roll dough to ⅛–¼ inch thick. Cut into desired shapes. Bake at 300°F for 25–35 minutes or until golden brown. These wild animals love to live in airtight containers for a long and crunchy life.

Variation: For a salty treat, brush rolled dough with olive oil, sprinkle with coarse-ground salt, and then cut into desired shapes.

High-Protein Leftovers Bread

makes 2 loaves

This is a heavy, savory bread that keeps well.

¼ cup canola *or* olive oil
2 teaspoons salt
4 cups leftover cooked vegetables and grains, mashed
    or strained, *or,* if you have no leftovers, 3 cups
    cooked millet and 1 cup cooked carrots or other
    vegetables, mashed or strained
5 cups whole wheat flour *or* 4 cups whole wheat plus
    1 cup rye flour
1 cup soy flour
vegetable stock *or* water, as needed
coarse cornmeal for dusting pans

In a large bowl, add oil and salt to the mashed vegetable-grain mixture and mix well. Combine flours and add to the bowl in three parts, first stirring, then mixing with your hands. If dough seems too dry to hold together, add a little warm water or stock to bring it to a "kneadable" consistency. Turn dough out onto floured surface and knead three hundred times (a great way to build those muscles for backpacking!), adding more flour to the kneading surface as necessary to prevent the dough from sticking. The dough should be smooth and springy.

    Divide dough in half and shape into loaves. Put into two oiled loaf pans (8 by 4½ by 3 inches) that have been sprinkled with cornmeal, and make a slit about ½ inch deep in the top of each loaf. Moisten the top with water, cover loaves with a kitchen towel, and place in a warm spot for 6 hours to overnight, depending on your time. This allows the bread to rise or "proof" without using yeast. Bake at 325°F for 1–1½ hours. Bread should be a medium-dark brown and sound hollow when thumped on the bottom. Remove from pans and allow to cool completely before packaging.

Breads & Crackers

Boston Brown Bread

==================================

makes 2 1-pound loaves

Smother this bread with cream cheese or nut butters for a delicious and filling lunch.

1 cup whole wheat flour
1 cup rye flour
1 cup cornmeal
2 teaspoons baking powder
1 teaspoon salt
2 cups buttermilk
⅔ cup molasses
1 cup raisins

Prepare two 1-pound coffee cans, or similar-size cans, by greasing and flouring to coat the insides well. Alternatively, line the cans with parchment paper. Set aside.

Combine dry ingredients. In a separate bowl, stir together buttermilk and molasses, and add with raisins to the flour mixture. Stir well to combine.

Turn mixture into the prepared coffee cans and cover each tightly with foil. Tie the foil securely with string. Place cans on a rack or trivet in a saucepan with a tight-fitting lid. Pour boiling water into saucepan, to come at least halfway up the sides of the coffee cans. Boil for 3 hours, adding boiling water to maintain the level.

Remove the can bottoms while the bread is still warm, and cool the cans on a rack. When the cans are cool, push out the bread and slice it into ½-inch slices. Pack the slices back into the cans and place plastic lids on each end. This makes crush-proof containers for hiking, and they are easily flattened to pack out.

Fruitcake

==

This is an excellent luxury snack for winter escapades. Slice thin and wrap each piece individually.

1 pound butter
2 cups honey
1 tablespoon cinnamon
1 tablespoon cloves
1 tablespoon nutmeg
1 tablespoon allspice
2 teaspoons mace
1 teaspoon ginger
1 teaspoon salt
4½ cups whole wheat flour
½ cup brandy *or* apple, orange, prune, *or* grape juice
2 pounds dried currants
2 pounds dried dates
½ pound raisins
1½ pounds walnuts, pecans, *or* hazelnuts

Cream butter and honey. Add spices and salt and stir well. Add flour alternately with ¼ cup brandy or fruit juice. Fold in the dried fruits and nuts. Line the bottoms of two oiled loaf pans with parchment or brown paper cut to fit. Oil the paper and pour in the cake batter. Place a shallow pan of water on the bottom shelf of the oven. Place loaf pans on the upper shelf and bake at 250°F for 3–3½ hours or until done. Bread should be medium-dark brown and sound hollow when thumped on the bottom. Remove from pans and cool.

Wrap the loaves in cheesecloth that has been dipped in brandy or juice, pour ¼ cup brandy or juice over the top, and wrap airtight in foil. If you want to make this months before you eat it, add ¼ cup brandy or fruit juice every couple of weeks or so. Just carefully open the foil, pour the liquid over the top, and reseal.

Boiled-Fruit Cake

———————————————————————————

makes 1 8-inch cake or 2 dozen muffins

An Australian favorite, this cake is boiled to plump up the fruit, then baked to finish.

4 cups dried fruit—raisins, golden raisins, currants,
    chopped apricots, peaches, prunes
1 cup water
¾ cup honey
1 cup butter
1 teaspoon baking soda
2 teaspoons cinnamon
½ teaspoon nutmeg
¼ teaspoon cloves
1 cup whole wheat flour
1 cup unbleached flour
2 teaspoons baking powder
1 egg, beaten

Preheat oven to 325°–350°F. Place the first eight ingredients together in a saucepan and bring to a simmer with the lid on. Simmer 5 minutes. Cool. Sift together flours and baking powder. Stir egg and flour into the fruit mixture. Mix to combine.

Turn into an 8-inch square pan greased with butter or lined with parchment paper. Bake for 1½ hours or until a cake tester comes out clean.

To bake as muffins, which are easier to pack and travel well, place batter in muffin papers in a muffin tin and bake at 325°–350°F for 25 minutes.

Dried Fruit Bread

============================

makes 3 small loaves

This heavy, sweet bread is high in protein. It's good for snacks with peanut butter and jam or toasted for breakfast with honey.

1 cup millet flour
3 cups rolled oats
1 cup dried apricots, chopped or cut with scissors
1 cup raisins
3 cups warm water
1 cup dates, pitted and chopped
1 cup mixed nuts, chopped
¼ cup honey
¼ cup canola oil
1 teaspoon anise seeds (optional)
¼ teaspoon salt
4–4¼ cups whole wheat flour
½ cup rye flour
½ cup soy flour
¼ cup milk powder

In a skillet over moderate heat, toast the millet flour, stirring constantly, until it is golden brown and has a toasty aroma. Set aside to cool. In a large bowl, soak the oats, apricots, and raisins in the warm water for 15 minutes. Add the dates, nuts, honey, oil, anise, and salt and mix well. Combine the flours with the milk powder and stir into the oat-fruit mixture a little at a time. As the dough thickens, you will need to use your hands. Turn dough out onto a floured surface and knead about three hundred times, kneading in extra wheat flour as needed to prevent sticking. Dough should be springy with a smooth texture.

Divide dough into three parts and form into loaves. Place them on an oiled cookie sheet and cut a ½-inch-deep slit in the top of each. Brush lightly with oil or water, cover with a kitchen towel, and set in a warm place for 6 hours to overnight, depending on your time. This allows the bread to rise or "proof" without the addition of yeast. Bake at 325°F for 1½ hours. Loaves should be medium-dark brown and sound hollow when thumped on the bottom. Cool thoroughly before packaging.

Sesame Seed Bread

makes 1 loaf

A little of this bread goes a long way, so slice it thin. The sweet, nutty flavor of the sesame comes out very well when the bread is toasted. It's a good accompaniment to soups.

1½ cups sesame seeds
1½ cups raw wheat germ
4 cups whole wheat flour
1 cup brown rice flour
1 cup millet flour
1½ teaspoons salt
1 tablespoon canola *or* olive oil
3 cups water

Toast sesame seeds and wheat germ separately in an ungreased frying pan, and combine in one bowl. Add flours and salt and mix well. Make a well in the center and add oil and water. Mix well. Spoon into a well-greased loaf pan (8 by 4½ by 3 inches). Bake at 325°F for 1¼ hours or until bread is golden brown and feels firm. Remove from pan and cool. For a soft crust, brush the top with a little oil while the bread is still hot.

Journey Cakes

Journey cakes are small patties made at home before the trip. They are packed with nutrition, easy to carry, and long lasting. Journey Cakes are great as a snack or combine well with soups, sauces, or condiments. Smothered in a piping-hot sauce, they work well as a quick dinner, perhaps combined with cheese or nuts. Eaten plain, they are a wonderful way to round out a meal without cooking on the trail.

Potato Cakes

===

Fresh potato flavor, moist and ready to eat out of your pack. For a full meal, serve with Miso Mustard Sauce (page 158) or plain mustard or horseradish. These are also good with Cream of Tomato Soup (page 136).

6 medium raw russet potatoes, grated, with peels
2 carrots, grated
2 onions, chopped
2 garlic cloves, minced
1 teaspoon mixed herbs (optional)
2 eggs, beaten
3 tablespoons melted butter
1 teaspoon salt
pinch of cayenne
1/4–1/2 cup whole wheat bread crumbs
1/2–1 cup Parmesan cheese (optional)

In a bowl, mix all ingredients thoroughly. Spread in an oiled 8-by-12-inch pan. Bake at 350°F for 1 hour. Cut into squares; cool. Wrap individually in waxed paper.

Food Processor Method: With the machine running, drop garlic through the feed tube to mince. Add onions and turn machine on and off several times to finely chop. Replace the blade with the shredding disk and shred the potatoes directly on top of the onions, using moderate pressure on the plunger. Set aside in a bowl. Replace the shredding disk with the blade, combine all the remaining ingredients, and add them to the reserved potato mixture. Mix and bake as above.

Polenta Cakes

==

makes 1 dozen

Polenta cakes are high-protein patties with the wonderful flavors of fresh vegetables. They are good accompaniments to soups or fried fish for dinner or with cheese for lunch and they always seem to be the first item out of your pack.

4 cups water
1 teaspoon salt
1 cup polenta *or* corn grits
2 tablespoons soy grits
2 onions, minced
2 carrots, grated
2 zucchini, grated
2 garlic cloves, minced
2 tablespoons olive oil
4 tablespoons sesame butter
½ cup sunflower seeds
3 tablespoons honey (optional)
1 tablespoon chia seeds (optional)
¼ cup milk powder (optional)

In a saucepan, bring water and salt to a boil. Stir in polenta and soy grits, bring back to a boil, cover, and reduce heat to low. Cook for 15–20 minutes. The mixture should be very thick. Remove from heat, stir well, and set aside until cool and firm. Meanwhile, sauté vegetables and garlic in oil until browned and dry. Remove from heat and stir in remaining ingredients. Cool. Combine the two mixtures well, until there are no lumps of polenta. Use your hands if need be. Form into 12 patties approximately 3 inches in diameter and ½ inch thick. Place on slightly greased cookie sheet and bake in moderate oven (350°F) for 30 minutes, turning once. The cakes will be brown and firm. Cool before packaging in plastic ziplock bag or lidded container.

Food Processor Method: With the machine running, drop garlic through the feed tube to mince. Add onions and pulse to finely chop. Replace the blade with the shredding disk and shred the carrots and zucchini directly on top of the onion. Follow the preceding directions.

Variations: Use nut butters in place of sesame butter; use leftover vegetables (mash them before adding); use nuts or pumpkin seeds in place of sunflower seeds; season with mixed herbs.

Pumpkin Pie Cakes

makes 1 dozen

These are a real treat for dessert. Spread them with cream cheese or eat them plain.

½ cup rolled oats
½ cup boiling water
1–1½ cups cooked pumpkin *or* yams
½ cup cornmeal
¼ cup maple syrup *or* honey
2 teaspoons cinnamon
1 teaspoon ginger
¼ teaspoon nutmeg
pinch of cloves *or* 1 tablespoon pumpkin pie spice
1 egg, lightly beaten

Cover oats in boiling water and let stand until water is absorbed. Cool. Combine the oats with remaining ingredients. Mix well. Drop from a spoon onto an oiled cookie sheet, and smooth out the tops with the back of the spoon. The cakes should be about 3 inches in diameter by ½ inch thick. Bake in a moderate oven (350°F) for 40 minutes, turning once. Cool. Wrap individually in waxed paper.

Carrot Cakes

━━━━━━━━━━━━━━━━━━━━━━━━━━━━

makes 15 squares

These are great on their own, or as a vegetable with dinner.

6 cups shredded carrots (about 10 medium carrots,
    or 1½ pounds)
1 small onion, chopped
2 garlic cloves, crushed
¼ cup whole wheat flour
½ cup whole wheat bread crumbs
2 eggs, beaten
1 cup freshly grated Parmesan cheese
grind of fresh pepper
pinch of nutmeg

Combine all ingredients and mix well. Spread into a greased 13-by-18-inch pan and cover with foil. Bake at 350°F for 45 minutes, remove foil, and bake for a further 15 minutes.

Cool pan on a rack, and cut into square cakes while warm. Remove cakes from pan when cold and wrap individually in waxed paper.

Food Processor Method: With the machine running, drop garlic through the feed tube to mince. Add onion and turn machine on and off several times to finely chop. Add bread crumbs and pulse the machine to combine. Add eggs, cheese, and seasonings, and turn on machine to combine. Replace the metal blade with the shredding disc and shred carrots directly on top of the egg mixture. Stir ingredients to combine and proceed as above.

Walnut Cheese Burgers

makes 1 dozen

These patties are rich and hearty. Serve them with Miso Mustard Sauce (page 158), or with soup for dinner. They're good plain out of your pack, too.

2 cups grated cheddar cheese
2 cups walnuts *or* pecans, ground
1 cup sesame seeds
½ cup sunflower seeds
½ cup raw wheat germ
½ cup minced fresh parsley
4 scallions, minced
3 large eggs

Combine all ingredients, beating in eggs to mix thoroughly. Form into 2½-by-½-inch patties and bake on a greased cookie sheet in a moderate oven (350°F) for 30 minutes, turning once, or sauté in a skillet. Cool before packing in a plastic ziplock bag or lidded container.

These patties can also be made in camp and served hot. Just mix all ingredients, except eggs, at home in a ziplock plastic bag. In camp, add the eggs, mix well, form into patties, and sauté.

Food Processor Method: With metal blade in place, finely chop parsley and scallions. Set aside. Grind nuts by turning the machine on and off until they are finely chopped. Add sesame and sunflower seeds, wheat germ, and eggs and pulse the machine to combine. Add to the scallions and parsley. Place the shredding disk on the machine and grate the cheese. Add to the reserved mixture, mix, and complete as above.

Soybean Burgers

==

makes 1 dozen

These patties have a hearty flavor that's good with cheese and mustard. You can also serve them with Marinara Sauce (page 152) or Mushroom Sauce (page 163).

1 cup dry soybeans, soaked overnight and cooked
     approximately 2 hours
1 onion, finely chopped
4 garlic cloves, minced
1 tablespoon minced fresh parsley
1 tablespoon olive oil
1 tablespoon miso
1 teaspoon tamari

Mash the beans well. Add remaining ingredients and mix well. The mash should be very thick and should hold well when shaped into a ball. Form into patties 3 inches in diameter and ½ inch thick and bake on a greased cookie sheet in a moderate oven (350°F) for about 30 minutes. Turn once while baking. Patties are done when they feel solid. They will be crusty on the outside and soft inside. Cool before packaging in plastic ziplock bags or a lidded container.

Food Processor Method: With the machine running, drop garlic through the feed tube to mince. Add parsley and turn the machine on and off several times to finely chop. Add cooked soybeans, turn the machine on and off a few times, and then let the machine run to mash the beans. Add remaining ingredients through the feed tube while the machine is running. Do not overprocess the beans to a paste. Then proceed as above.

Variations: Add a grated carrot; season with 1 teaspoon cumin and ½ teaspoon chili powder; season with oregano.

Falafel

Serve this spicy Middle Eastern snack in pocket bread with slices of cucumber and Tahini Dipping Sauce (page 81), or eat it out of your pack along the trail.

2 cups garbanzo beans
½ cup each chopped celery and scallions
3 garlic cloves, minced
2 teaspoons cumin seeds, crushed
1 teaspoon coriander seeds, crushed
½ teaspoon ground turmeric
¼ teaspoon cayenne
2 eggs
3 tablespoons sesame tahini
1 tablespoon lemon juice

Soak the beans for a few hours and drain. In a saucepan, cover soaked beans generously with fresh water. Bring to a boil, reduce heat to low, cover, and simmer gently for 2–2½ hours. Drain. Blend the beans in a blender or food processor until smooth or mash them well with a potato masher. Combine with the remaining ingredients and blend until evenly mixed. Chill for at least an hour.

With floured hands, shape into balls the size of a walnut. Dust each ball with flour or fine bread crumbs. Deep-fry at 365°F until golden brown, or shape into 1½-inch-diameter patties and sauté. Cool. Carry in a lidded plastic container.

Lentil Rice Cakes

----

makes 1 dozen

These protein-rich cakes are good alone, or serve them with Tahini Dipping Sauce (page 81).

⅔ cup brown rice
⅓ cup lentils
1 teaspoon salt
3 cups water
1 small onion, finely chopped
1 small carrot, grated
2 garlic cloves, minced
1 tablespoon minced fresh parsley
1 tablespoon olive oil
1 teaspoon tamari

Season with *one* of the following:
2–4 teaspoons cumin
2–4 teaspoons curry power

In a saucepan, bring the rice, lentils, salt, and water to a boil, cover, and reduce heat to low. Cook 50–60 minutes. The mixture should be dry, with all water absorbed. Allow to cool. Mash well with your hands, then add remaining ingredients, and mix well. Form into 3-inch-diameter patties, ½ inch thick. Place on a greased cookie sheet, and bake at 350°F for 30–45 minutes, turning once. Cool before packaging in plastic ziplock bag or lidded container.

Food Processor Method: Chop onion, carrot, parsley, and garlic finely with metal blade; add oil and tamari. Add the dry rice and lentil mixture and pulse several times to combine, but don't overprocess to a paste. Then proceed as above.

Brown Rice Cakes

===================================

These are good for lunch with cheddar cheese or as an accompaniment to fish. Sprinkle with soy sauce or spread mustard on top if desired.

1 cup brown rice
3 cups water
1 teaspoon salt
1 carrot, grated
1 onion, finely chopped
½–1 cup chopped spinach, mustard greens,
    watercress, *or* arugula
1 tablespoon olive oil
2 teaspoons ground ginger

In a saucepan, bring rice, water, and salt to a boil. Cover, reduce heat to low, and cook 60 minutes. Allow to cool. Mash well with your hands, add remaining ingredients, and continue to mix and mash with your hands. If mixture is too moist, add a little soy flour. Form into 3-inch patties, ½ inch thick, and bake on a greased cookie sheet at 350°F for 30 minutes, turning once. Cool before packaging in plastic ziplock bag or lidded container.

Food Processor Method: Mash the cooked rice and remaining ingredients by pulsing. Scrape down the bowl occasionally. Do not overprocess to a paste. Then proceed as above.

Oriental Brown Rice Cakes

================================

makes 1 dozen

A good accompaniment to Spicy Hot and Sour Soup (page 131), these cakes are also tasty when dipped in Sweet and Sour Sauce (page 154).

1 cup brown rice
2½ cups water
1 teaspoon salt
1 carrot, grated
2 garlic cloves, minced
1 tablespoon toasted sesame oil
1 teaspoon freshly grated gingerroot
2 tablespoons fermented black beans, chopped
    (optional)

In a saucepan, bring rice, water, and salt to a boil. Cover, reduce heat to low, and cook for 40–60 minutes. Cool. Add remaining ingredients and mash well with your hands. Form into 3-inch patties, ½ inch thick, and bake on an oiled cookie sheet at 350°F for 30–45 minutes, turning once. Cool on a rack before packaging in a plastic ziplock bag or lidded container.

Food Processor Method: Pulse the cooked rice and remaining ingredients. Scrape down the bowl occasionally. Do not overprocess to a paste. Then proceed as above.

Millet Seed Cakes

makes 1 dozen

Serve these cakes for dinner with Cream of Tomato Soup (page 136) or a mild broth. They are a spicy treat.

1 cup millet
2 garlic cloves, crushed
1 carrot, finely chopped
2½ cups water
¼ cup sesame seeds
6 cardamom pods, husks removed
1 teaspoon coriander
1 teaspoon cinnamon
½ teaspoon fennel seeds
¼ cup fenugreek
salt and pepper to taste

Bring millet, garlic, carrot, and water to a boil. Cook for 3 minutes, then reduce heat to low, cover, and simmer for 20 minutes. Meanwhile, grind the seeds and spices (except salt and pepper) together with mortar and pestle, coffee grinder, or electric mill till finely ground. When the millet has cooked, stir in the seeds, spices, salt, and pepper, and mash well with a potato masher. Allow to cool enough so you can handle the mixture. Shape into cakes 3 inches in diameter and ½ inch thick. Place on an oiled cookie sheet and bake at 350°F for 30 minutes, turning once. Cool on a rack before packaging in plastic ziplock bag or lidded container.

Millet Date Orange Cakes

These sweet orange-scented cakes are a tasty quick snack.

1 cup millet
2½ cups water
1 cup dates, pitted and chopped
rind of 1 orange, grated
1 cup walnuts, finely chopped
2–3 tablespoons honey
2 tablespoons canola *or* walnut oil

In a saucepan, bring millet and water to a boil. Reduce heat to low, cover, and cook for 20 minutes. Mash with a potato masher to a paste. When millet is cool enough to handle, add dates, orange rind, walnuts, honey, and oil. Mix well. Shape into cakes 3 inches in diameter and ½ inch thick and bake on an oiled cookie sheet at 350°F for 30 minutes or until brown on both sides. Turn once. Cool cakes on a wire rack before packaging in plastic ziplock bag or lidded container.

Coconut Almond Barley Cakes

makes 1 dozen

This is a sweet Journey Cake that is wonderful spread with nut butter or just eaten plain.

¼ cup barley
3 cups water
½ cup blanched toasted almonds, chopped fine (toast in 350°F oven for 8 minutes)
¼ cup unsweetened shredded or macaroon coconut
1 tablespoon honey
grating of fresh nutmeg

In a saucepan, bring barley and water to a boil and cook for 3 minutes. Reduce heat to low, cover, and cook for about 1 hour. Cool. Mash with the remaining ingredients using your hands and combine well. Shape into patties 3 inches in diameter and ½ inch thick and bake on an oiled cookie sheet at 350°F for 20–30 minutes, or until firm and brown. Turn once. Cool on a rack. Wrap when cold in waxed paper or plastic wrap.

Food Processor Method: Cook the barley as above. Then pulse it and the remaining ingredients with the metal blade to combine, scraping down the bowl. Do not overprocess to a paste. Then proceed as above.

Seed Cakes

This is a different-tasting cake, good with peanut butter and honey, cheese, hot mustard, any sauce or gravy, or just plain.

2 cups water
½ teaspoon salt
½ cup polenta *or* corn grits
2 tablespoons soy grits
1 cup sunflower seeds
½ cup pumpkin seeds
2 tablespoons sesame seeds
2 tablespoons chia seeds (optional)
1 teaspoon honey (optional)

In a saucepan, bring water and salt to a boil. Stir in polenta and soy grits and bring back to a boil. Cover, reduce heat to low, and cook until very thick, 15–20 minutes. Cool. Meanwhile, grind all the seeds except the chia seeds and a few sunflower seeds. When the polenta mixture is cool, add all the seeds and the honey. Mix well with your hands, and form into patties approximately 3 inches in diameter and ½ inch thick. Bake on a greased cookie sheet in a moderate oven (350°F) for 30 minutes, turning once. Cool before packaging in plastic ziplock bag or lidded container.

Food Processor Method: Follow the preceding directions but combine the cooked polenta and remaining ingredients in the processor, with the metal blade, turning the machine on and off until the mixture is uniform. Proceed as above.

Spreads, Dressings & Condiments

Prepare these before you go, eliminating extra mess in camp. The spreads are good for any meal, especially lunch, when you might not want to cook. Toss the dressings into warm pasta, rice, or bulgur.

Sesame Butter Spread

makes ½ cup

This spread is great on crackers.

½ cup raw sesame butter
dash of salt
¼–1 teaspoon grated orange peel to taste

Roast sesame butter and salt in a frying pan over medium heat until brown, stirring constantly, 5–10 minutes. Add orange peel when cool. Carry in a lidded plastic container.

Miso Spread

makes approximately ¾ cup

Use this as a thin spread on breads or Journey Cakes (page 60), with or without sliced cheese. It's easy to make in camp, too.

4–6 garlic cloves, minced
1 teaspoon olive oil (to just cover bottom of pan)
¼ cup sesame *or* peanut butter
1 tablespoon plus 1 teaspoon miso
½ cup water

Sauté garlic in oil over medium heat, stirring lightly, until the garlic turns translucent. Mix the sesame or peanut butter and miso, and add them and the water to the pan. Stir until thick. Carry in a lidded plastic container.

Variations: Serve a small amount of spread with rice or another grain for extra flavor and nourishment.

Miso Sesame Butter Spread

makes approximately ¾ cup

This is a high-protein, quick-energy spread. It's good for lunch on crackers, cold leftover pancakes, or bread.

¾ cup sesame butter
2 tablespoons miso
2–3 tablespoons boiling water
¼–1 teaspoon grated orange peel to taste

Brown sesame butter and miso in a frying pan over moderate heat for about 2 minutes, stirring constantly. Add water and mix to spreading consistency. Cool and add orange peel. Carry in a lidded plastic container.

Garlic Spread

makes approximately ¼ cup

This spread is good on bread, with spaghetti or chili, or alone when you get a garlic craving. You can make it in camp, too.

12–15 large garlic cloves, coarsely chopped
⅓ cup water
1 tablespoon butter *or* olive oil

Combine garlic and water in a saucepan and bring to a boil. Lower heat and simmer for 10–15 minutes. Add butter or oil and stir well. Carry in a lidded plastic container.

Sweet Mixed Seed Butter

makes approximately 1¾ cups

Use this on bread, crackers, or sweet Journey Cakes (page 60), or add a little more water and spread it on pancakes.

½ cup pumpkin seeds
½ cup sunflower seeds
¼ cup sesame butter
2 tablespoons honey
1 tablespoon oil
1 tablespoon water (approximately)

In a seed grinder or blender, grind pumpkin and sunflower seeds with enough water to make them spreadable. Then combine all the ingredients in a bowl and mix well. Carry in a lidded plastic container.

Variations: To make a Salty Mixed Seed Butter, follow the same recipe, but replace honey with 2 teaspoons miso and increase the amount of water to approximately 3 tablespoons.

Citrus Cream Cheese Spread

makes ½ cup

Spread on cakes, crackers, breads, or pancakes.

½ cup cream cheese
rind of 1 lemon *or* orange, grated
1–2 tablespoons honey

Mix ingredients well. Carry in a plastic lidded container.

Miso Dressing

makes approximately ¼ cup

It's easy to mix up a small amount of salad dressing before you go, put it in a jar, and carry it in your pack, ready to use. This recipe has added nourishment because of the miso, and it keeps well.

1 tablespoon each miso, olive oil, water, lemon juice
1 garlic clove, sliced
1 teaspoon whole oregano, thyme, or basil

Mix all ingredients well. Carry in a small airtight bottle, and shake well before using.

Cilantro Lime Dressing

makes 1 cup

This fresh-tasting and zingy dressing is a wonderful treat on the trail. It tastes great on a Burrito (see page 209) or on cool pasta as a salad with pine nuts.

4 garlic cloves
2 cups cilantro, cleaned and stemmed
¼ cup lime juice
½ cup olive oil
salt and pepper to taste

With the food processor running, add garlic through the feed tube to mince. Turn machine off, add cilantro and lime juice, then pulse to a paste. With machine running, drizzle in olive oil. Add salt and pepper. Shake well before using.

Sesame Butter Dressing

makes ¼ cup

Salad dressings taste really good in the mountains. Make a pot of noodles, drain, add lots of dried parsley and onions, remove from the heat, and toss in some dressing. Also use this dressing with boiled or baked potatoes, adding some dill or other herbs.

1 tablespoon sesame butter
2–3 tablespoons water
1 teaspoon tamari
1 teaspoon lemon juice
½ teaspoon chervil, dill, *or* tarragon

Put all ingredients in a small airtight bottle. Shake well before using.

Variation: Use 1 tablespoon peanut butter instead.

Mustardy Vinaigrette

makes ½ cup

Toss this dressing with warm pasta, rice, bulgur, or fresh grated vegetables.

½ cup olive oil
2 tablespoons vinegar (balsamic, red wine, or rice)
1 shallot *or* onion
4 teaspoons Dijon mustard
⅛ teaspoon tarragon
salt and pepper to taste

Put ingredients in a blender or food processor and blend until smooth. Carry in an airtight plastic bottle. Shake well before using.

Lemon Tahini Dressing

makes ¾ cup

Toss with warm pasta, instant wild rice, or cooked mung beans and chopped nuts.

¼ cup lemon juice
3 tablespoons olive oil
2 tablespoons sesame tahini
1 tablespoon tamari
1 tablespoon water
1 garlic clove
pinch each of celery seed, salt, pepper

Put ingredients in a blender or food processor and blend until smooth. Carry in an airtight plastic bottle. Shake well before using.

Tahini Dipping Sauce

makes ½ cup

This is great over Falafel (page 67) or as a sauce for other Journey Cakes (page 60) or fresh vegetables.

¼ cup sesame tahini
4 tablespoons lemon juice
3 garlic cloves, crushed *or* minced fine
1 teaspoon cilantro
pinch of salt
3–4 tablespoons water

Combine all ingredients and mix well. Package in a lidded plastic container.

Home-Dried Mushrooms

Gently dust off mushrooms with a soft brush (there are brushes specifically for cleaning mushrooms) and wipe lightly with a damp towel. String a needle with heavy thread and push the needle through the center of each mushroom from top to bottom. Hang horizontally in a warm, dry area until dry—about 3 days. Be sure the mushrooms don't touch. If you are using larger mushrooms, slice them about ½ inch thick, string as above, putting the needle through sideways, and dry the same way. For a quicker option, place clean, sliced mushrooms on a clean cooling rack and dry in an oven at the lowest setting with the door slightly ajar. Turn as needed during drying. The drying time might take up to 24 hours, depending on size and the amount of moisture in the mushrooms. Or dry them in a dehydrator; follow the manufacturer's instructions.

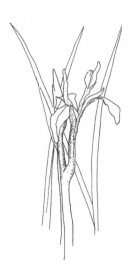

Wakame

serves 2

This is a seaweed condiment for rice or other grains.

¼ cup dried wakame, cut in ½-inch lengths
2 tablespoons onion flakes
½ cup water
1 teaspoon oil

Soak wakame and onion flakes in the water for 15 minutes. Strain and reserve the liquid. Put the oil in a frying pan, add the seaweed and onion flakes, and stir-fry for a few minutes. Add the reserved liquid and bring to a boil. Reduce heat and cook 5–10 minutes.

Garnishes: ¾ teaspoon lemon juice; ¾ teaspoon tamari; ¾ teaspoon miso paste.

Popped Seeds

makes 1 cup

Add these seeds to soup for extra crunch or eat by the handful as a snack.

Heat a pan over moderate heat and add 1 cup, mixed or by themselves: hulled pumpkin seeds, sunflower seeds, squash seeds. Toast lightly, stirring constantly. When all seem to have popped or browned, add 1–2 teaspoons soy sauce per cup of seeds and stir well and quickly, because the sauce will crystallize rapidly. Put in a bowl or on a plate and let cool a bit before eating.

Basil Salt

This is an aromatic salt to sprinkle. Don't be limited to basil—try any herb or combination. To *1 part of basil or other herbs,* add *2 parts of sea salt.* Grind them together in a coffee grinder or blender or with mortar and pestle, or roll them with a rolling pin to crush. Carry in a shaker bottle.

Sesame Salt

makes approximately 1 cup

Known as *gomasio* to some, this wonderful garnish not only heightens flavor, but also adds the valuable food energy of the sesame seed. In a short time you will find yourself sprinkling it on everything on which you ever used plain salt.

1¼ cups sesame seeds, unhulled
1 tablespoon sea salt (or to taste)

Roast sesame seeds in a dry frying pan over moderate heat, stirring constantly until the seeds darken and begin to pop, about 5 minutes. Then combine the seeds with the salt. Grind with mortar and pestle, coffee grinder, or blender. Store in an airtight container.

Fresh Foods

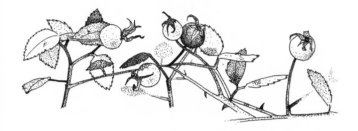

You've been pulling yourself up that switchback for what seems like a lifetime. But you know what awaits you at the top: your favorite campsite, a beautiful sunset, and those juicy organic oranges you bought at the farmers' market before the trip. As you sit on that old familiar boulder, thoughts of the Skillet Bake (page 87) you brought for dinner begin to move you toward the camp kitchen. Potatoes, mushrooms, onions, garlic, pecans, and cheddar cheese are all wrapped and ready to just heat up in the pan. Serve with sliced cucumbers tossed in Cilantro Lime Dressing (page 79), and your first-night meal on the trail will give you a taste of home.

Fresh Vegetable Soup

Fresh homemade soup in camp is a luxury worth the extra weight carried on that first day's hike.

Check the fridge. There's always something that won't keep until you get back, and often it's a vegetable or two. So we have come up with a delicious way to use them on the first day or two of your trip.

At Home: Grate the heavier vegetables that will hold up—such as carrots, beets, turnips, rutabagas, parsnips, yams, and burdock root—and store them in a plastic ziplock bag. Cabbage can be carried whole or cut in sections. Little red or small Yukon gold potatoes, cut in half and steamed, will hold up for a couple days. Greens (spinach, kale) can be chopped and sautéed, then cooled and packed in ziplock plastic bags. Any fresh herbs, such as parsley, oregano, rosemary, sage, chives, dill, etc., can be chopped, spread loosely on a cookie sheet, and toasted in a very low-heat oven for about 10 minutes. Cooked rice can be put in a ziplock bag and used that first night. Such a good feeling to use up what you have!

In Camp: Sauté the potatoes or rice in a little olive oil with some chopped fresh onion. Add water, a variety of fresh vegetables (use your imagination!), salt or soy sauce, and a bouillon of your choice. Season with your favorite herb and cook until done, probably no more than 5 minutes. Keep covered and let sit 5 minutes. Sprinkle a grated dry cheese (Parmesan, dry jack, cheddar), popped seeds, or toasted nuts on top and enjoy.

Skillet Bake

Here's a great meal for the first night out. Use your imagination, have fun, and enjoy.

At Home: Sauté, roast, or steam some of your favorite vegetables and combine with herbs, spices, nuts, and cheeses. Place mixture in double ziplock bags to prevent leakage. Bring enough heavy-duty foil to wrap and seal the contents for baking in camp.

In Camp: Remove vegetable mixture from plastic bag and seal in foil. Place foil packet in skillet over medium heat. Let the meal "bake" for 10–15 minutes, unwrap, and serve.

Some combos to consider:

- sauté eggplant, mushrooms, onions, garlic, basil, and oregano in olive oil; add walnuts, Parmesan and Monterey Jack cheese, and toss together

- sauté zucchini, roasted red peppers, onions, garlic, red pepper flakes, and oregano in olive oil; add mozzarella cheese and toss together

- steam or roast yams, parsnips, rutabaga, carrots, golden beets, yucca root, burdock root (shredded), and turnips until done; pour into a bowl and stir in fresh chopped parsley, garlic, olive oil, and roasted pine nuts

Potatoes & Mushrooms

Cook the potatoes, mushrooms, onions, and garlic at home, mix with the remaining ingredients, and heat up in camp. It's easy and comforting

2 potatoes (with skins), boiled and chopped
2 cups chopped and sautéed mushrooms
1 onion, chopped and sautéed (optional)
½ cup chopped pecans
2 garlic cloves, sliced
2 tablespoons butter
parsley *or* mixed herbs to taste
salt and pepper to taste
cheddar cheese to taste, grated or cubed

At Home: Combine ingredients except cheese, and place in a ziplock plastic bag. Dot with butter and seal well.

In Camp: Empty contents of the bag into a frying pan and cook, covered, over moderate heat for 5–10 minutes. Stir in the cheese and serve.

Variations: Blend in 1 tablespoon of vermouth before packaging. Also try this recipe with yams.

Stuffed Portobello

================================

serves 2

Portobello mushrooms have become the "steak" of vegetarians. This full-flavored fungi, coupled with Greens and Quick-Cooking Pasta or Quinoa (page 92), may be eaten on the first or second night out. Tastes like mushroom pizza without the crust.

1 large portobello mushroom with stem
¼ teaspoon each dried oregano, parsley, and thyme
⅛ teaspoon Asian chili (optional)
¼ teaspoon salt
1 garlic clove, minced
2 tablespoons olive oil, combined with 2 tablespoons
    butter
3 ounces white cheddar cheese, grated
1 or 2 sun-dried tomatoes, chopped (optional)

At Home: Carefully remove stem from portobello cap and dice. Combine with the herbs, chili, salt, and minced garlic and sauté, using half the oil-butter mixture, until stem is soft. Set aside to cool. Add half the grated cheese, and mix. Package in an airtight bag. If you are using sun-dried tomatoes, soak them in ¼ cup hot water for 10 minutes, drain, slice thin, and add them to the stem mixture. Package the portobello cap and remaining half of the grated cheese in separate ziplock bags. Carry the remaining half of the oil-butter mixture in another container.

In Camp: In a skillet, sauté the portobello cap over medium heat in the remaining oil-butter mixture. Turn the mushroom often, keeping the pan covered in between. When the portobello begins to soften, fill it with the stem mixture and sprinkle on the remaining cheese. Add a few tablespoons of water to the skillet and cook, covered, until the cheese is melted. Cut in half and serve.

Mashed Potatoes & Greens

serves 4

Greens, cooked at home and then added to mashed potatoes and cheese in camp, taste like down-home comfort food! This recipe is delicious as a side vegetable and makes a complete meal served with fried fish or a seafood sausage.

1 medium onion, chopped
2 tablespoons olive oil
1 bunch greens (spinach, chard, etc.), chopped
soy sauce *or* salt to taste
1½ cups instant mashed potatoes
3 tablespoons milk powder
2 tablespoons butter *or* olive oil
cheddar cheese, grated (optional)

At Home: Sauté onion in olive oil until soft. Add the greens and sauté until they are wilted. Sprinkle with soy sauce or salt, stir, and set aside. When cool, store in a ziplock bag in the refrigerator to chill just before you put them in your pack. Package instant potatoes, milk powder, butter, and cheddar cheese in a separate bag.

In Camp: Heat *2½ cups* of water to a simmer. Remove from heat and stir in potatoes, milk powder, and butter until completely mixed and thick. Add greens and stir. Sprinkle grated cheddar on top and stir in. So easy and comforting.

Tempeh & Onions

================================

serves 4

Tempeh is a wonderful soybean product. Used in abundance in Zen monasteries, especially in the winter, it is an inexpensive and easy way to get protein. This recipe, accompanied by rice (particularly Mushroom Rice, page 183), is hearty and wonderful. Try it on a cold or rainy night.

1 large onion
2 tablespoons olive oil
1 tablespoon butter
1 8-ounce package tempeh, plain or flavored
1 tablespoon soy sauce

At Home: Pack all ingredients separately. To make tempeh last longer, place it in an airtight bag and freeze it before putting it in your pack.

In Camp: Peel onion and cut in half lengthwise. With cut sides down, slice crosswise into ⅓-inch pieces. Then cut those slices in half. Sauté them in the olive oil and butter over medium heat until they turn light brown, not completely caramelized, but soft and brown, about 5 minutes. Stir often and watch carefully. Cut the block of tempeh into bite-size pieces and sauté with onions, stirring often. Cook another 3–4 minutes over medium-low heat. Add soy sauce and stir quickly to coat everything with the sauce. Serve immediately.

Fresh Foods

91

Greens & Quick-Cooking Pasta or Quinoa

serves 4

Cooking up greens at home and creating a meal around them in camp on the first night or two helps to round out a day of granola, trail mix, cheese, crackers, and nuts! This recipe is meant to inspire you to incorporate greens into a variety of meal possibilities—add them to marinara sauce, sauté them into scrambled eggs, stir them into a soup, or enjoy them as a side dish. The options are endless!

1 cup sun-dried tomatoes
1 large onion, sliced
1 teaspoon Asian chili flakes (optional)
4 tablespoons olive oil
4 garlic cloves, minced
1 teaspoon each dried thyme and oregano *or* 1
    tablespoon dried basil
1 pound greens (spinach, chard, kale, etc.), washed
    and chopped small (remove hard ribs and thick
    stems)
2 tablespoons capers (optional)
2 tablespoons pine nuts (optional)
1 pound pasta or 2 cups quinoa
grated Parmesan cheese

At Home: Cover tomatoes with hot water and let soak for 10–15 minutes. Sauté onion and chili flakes in olive oil until the onions are soft and start to get some color. Add garlic and herbs and stir quickly. Add greens and cook about 5 minutes, stirring often. Toss in the capers and/or pine nuts. Cool. Package mixture in two ziplock bags (double up) or in a plastic container inside a ziplock bag. Carry in a cool spot in your pack and eat the first day out.

Fresh Foods

In Camp: To conserve fuel, fine noodles may be cooked by pouring boiling (salted) water over them, covering them, and then wrapping the pot in a blanket or towel. Allow to sit for 10 minutes, then drain. To cook quinoa, bring to a boil the (salted) water and quinoa (two parts water to one part quinoa), then lower heat and simmer for 5 minutes. Turn heat off, cover, and let sit 15 minutes. Serve with Parmesan cheese on top.

Simple Garden for the Pack

Fresh greens are great in Burritos (page 209), on top of a Journey Cake (page 60), or with a little dressing as a side salad.

1 1-quart Nalgene or other wide-mouth plastic bottle
    with lid
1 6–8-inch square of nylon screen
rubber band or string
2 tablespoons sprouting seeds: alfalfa, radish, lentil,
    fenugreek, sunflower

At Home: Begin the sprouting a day or two before you hit the trail. Place seeds in the bottle with enough water to cover them, and let soak overnight. Next day, remove the lid and place the screen over the bottle mouth and secure with rubber band or string. Drain seeds and rinse. Cover with water once again.

In Camp: Continue to rinse and drain the seeds once a day. Watch your garden grow! Be sure to keep the sprouts in a dark place in your pack. If there is any doubt about water purity, boil water, cool, and use it to rinse.

3

Foods to Make in Camp

Planning and prepackaging individual meals at home before the trip allows you to control the ingredients with health and variety in mind, keeps costs down, and gives you the freedom to prepare simple and quick meals in camp. Don't forget to adjust cooking times for your particular stove, cookware, and camp elevation.

Cereals

Carrying a pack while hiking through the wilderness uses a lot of energy, and a good breakfast will help to keep your endurance up. High-protein grains, nuts, seeds, and dried fruits all appear in these energizing breakfast-cereal recipes.

Seed Cereal

==

makes approximately 2½ cups

This is good by itself with cold or warm milk, or served with Stewed Fruit Sauce (page 167). It may also be used as a high-protein garnish for hot cereals.

1 cup almonds
½ cup pumpkin seeds
½ cup sunflower seeds
¼ cup date sugar
2 tablespoons carob powder (optional)

At Home: Grind nuts and seeds, and combine them with remaining ingredients. Store in an airtight container.

In Camp: Serve as a cereal or use as a topping for hot cereals, soups, or stewed fruit or as added nourishment in one-pot meals.

Soaked Cereal

==================================

serves 2–3

Wake up to breakfast in bed with this satisfying no-cook cereal.

1 cup rolled oats
1 cup rolled wheat
raisins, to taste
unsweetened coconut, to taste
dried apples, chopped, to taste

At Home: Combine ingredients in a ziplock plastic bag.

In Camp: The night before, empty contents of package into your cook pot. Stir in *3 cups* of cold water, cover, and set aside until morning. Serve cold, or warm it up over low heat, stirring frequently. Sweeten to taste.

Variations: Add chopped nuts; add dried apricots, dates, or other fruit; mix ⅔ cup milk powder with water and add; add cinnamon or other spices; try with rolled barley or rye; add sesame or sunflower seeds.

Bird Seed Cereal

This cereal has the unique flavor of raw whole grains. The texture is crunchy and chewy.

¼ cup rolled oats
¼ cup millet
¼ cup milk powder
¼ cup almonds *or* filberts, chopped
2 tablespoons rolled wheat
2 tablespoons toasted buckwheat groats
small handful of raisins, chopped dates, and
      sunflower seeds
pinch of salt
date sugar (optional)

At Home: Combine ingredients in a ziplock plastic bag.

In Camp: The night before, empty contents of bag into your cook pot and stir in *1 cup* of water. Cover and set aside. In the morning, serve the cereal cold or warm it up over low heat, stirring frequently.

Cold Morning Wheat Cereal

serves 2

The dried fruit makes this cereal sweet, and the butter helps keep you warm.

1 cup finely cracked wheat *or* bulgur
¼ cup milk powder
½ teaspoon salt
handful of raisins *or* pitted dates
handful of walnuts
2 tablespoons butter

At Home: Combine ingredients in a ziplock plastic bag.

In Camp: Bring *4 cups* of water to a boil. Stir in the contents of the bag and return to a boil. Cover, remove from heat, and let stand for 5–10 minutes or until tender.

Variations: This can also be made with cracked-wheat cereals, available in natural food stores.

Hot Cracked Millet Cream Cereal

serves 2

This is a good winter cereal, high in protein and a source of calcium and iron. It's delicious.

½ cup cracked millet
⅔ cup dates
⅔ cup black walnuts, filberts, *or* almonds, coarsely
     chopped
¼ teaspoon salt
2 teaspoons oil *or* butter (optional)
unsweetened coconut, to taste (optional)

At Home: In a skillet over moderate heat, toast millet until it's golden brown. Put it in a blender and crack but do not grind it. Cool. Combine with remaining ingredients in a ziplock bag.

In Camp: Bring *2 cups* of water to a boil. Slowly stir in contents of the bag. Cook 8–10 minutes, stirring frequently.

Quinoa & Fruit Cereal

This warm, sweet, slightly tart breakfast cereal includes some favorite fruits. It also would be good for dessert on a cold night.

½ cup quinoa
⅛ teaspoon salt
½ cup dried fruit (apples, apricots, raisins, cherries, cranberries, etc.)
pinch of cinnamon (optional)
¼ cup chopped toasted walnuts, pecans, almonds, *or* hazelnuts
juice from ½ lemon

At Home: Place quinoa, salt, dried fruit, and cinnamon in one airtight plastic bag. Put nuts in a separate bag. Carry the lemon in your Staples for the Stuff Sack bag (see page 13).

In Camp: Combine all ingredients except nuts and bring to a boil in *1 cup* of water. Reduce heat and simmer for 15 minutes. Turn off heat, stir in nuts, and serve with maple syrup poured on top.

Rice Cream Cereal

———————————————————

serves 2

This delicate cereal is good for small children.

½ cup brown rice flour

At Home: In a skillet over moderate heat, toast flour until it's golden brown. Cool and package in a ziplock plastic bag.

In Camp: Empty flour into your cook pot. Stir in 2 *cups* of water, bring to a boil, and cook for 5 minutes. Serve with butter and honey.

Toasted Oatmeal

———————————————————

serves 2

Eat your oats!

1 cup rolled oats
¼ teaspoon salt

In Camp: Toast oats in cook pot or skillet over medium heat, stirring constantly. When oats are golden brown and have a toasted aroma, add 3 *cups* of water and the salt, reduce heat to low, and simmer 5 minutes. Serve with dates, raisins, nuts, butter, or your favorite topping.

Rice Pudding

Children love this age-old warm cereal recipe. And some big people do, too!

2 cups cooked rice (basmati, brown, jasmine)
dash of cloves
¼ teaspoon ground nutmeg
¼ teaspoon cinnamon
dash of salt
½ teaspoon vanilla (optional)
½ cup raisins, currants, *or* chopped apples
½ cup chopped walnuts (optional)
2 tablespoons milk powder

At Home: If you're not planning to use leftover rice for this dish, cook 1 cup rice in 2 cups water according to the directions for the type of rice you are using. Cool and package in an airtight bag. Combine spices, salt, vanilla, dried fruit, and walnuts in a ziplock bag. Put milk powder in a separate bag. Carry maple syrup or honey in your Staples for the Stuff Sack bag (see page 13).

In Camp: Combine *2 cups* of water in a pot with rice and fruit-spice mixture, and simmer, covered, for 10 minutes, stirring occasionally. Dissolve milk powder in *¼ cup* of water and add to rice pot. Stir over low heat until cereal reaches desired consistency, about 3–5 minutes. Top with maple syrup or honey.

Pancakes

Pancakes are good on slow mornings, when you feel like sitting in the sun on a granite boulder with a cup of hot tea, letting the warmth soak in after a frosty night. Cook extra pancakes and serve them as bread for lunch.

Oatmeal Hotcakes

serves 2

These are good on those mornings when you want to eat a lot. They are sweet and filling.

2 cups rolled oatmeal
½ cup milk powder
¼ teaspoon cinnamon
¼ teaspoon nutmeg
¼ teaspoon salt
¼ cup date sugar (optional)
¼ cup currants *or* raisins
1 tablespoon sesame seeds
1 teaspoon baking powder
2 tablespoons oil
1 egg (optional)

At Home: Whir the oats in a blender or food processor until most of them reach a flourlike consistency. Leave some in small pieces. Then combine with the dry ingredients and package in a ziplock plastic bag. Carry egg and oil separately.

In Camp: Combine contents of bag with the oil, optional egg, and 1¼ *cups* of water. Let the mixture stand at least 10 minutes before gently cooking the pancakes in a hot oiled pan to a golden brown. Serve with butter and honey. Leftovers are great to snack on.

Corn Pancakes

==

serves 2

These go well with peanut butter and maple syrup or
Stewed Fruit Sauce (page 167).

¾ cup corn flour or cornmeal
¾ cup whole wheat flour
½ cup raw wheat germ
½ cup milk powder
2 teaspoons baking powder
½ teaspoon salt
2 tablespoons oil *or* butter
1 tablespoon honey (optional)

At Home: Combine ingredients in a ziplock plastic bag.

In Camp: Empty contents of bag into a pot or bowl.
Stir in *1½ cups* of water. Cook pancakes in a hot oiled
pan. Save leftovers for lunch.

Whole Wheat Soy Pancakes

serves 2

These are good, heavy, energy-boosting pancakes, very high in protein. They come out dark and are delicious with maple syrup.

2 cups whole wheat flour
½ cup soy flour
½ cup raw wheat germ
½ cup milk powder
2 teaspoons baking powder
1 teaspoon salt
2 tablespoons oil

At Home: Combine ingredients in a ziplock plastic bag.

In Camp: Empty contents of bag into a bowl or pot. Stir in *2 cups* of water. Cook pancakes in a hot oiled pan.

Brown Rice Flour Pancakes

These light, mellow pancakes are good with Sesame Butter Spread (page 76) and honey or maple syrup.

2 cups brown rice flour
⅓ cup milk powder
2 teaspoons baking powder
½ teaspoon salt
2 tablespoons honey
2 tablespoons oil

At Home: Combine ingredients in a ziplock plastic bag.

In Camp: Empty contents of bag into a bowl or pot. Stir in *1 cup* of water. Cook pancakes in a hot oiled pan.

Buckwheat Pancakes

serves 2–4

Buckwheat is a great source of protein, which will help replenish your energy. Serve with lots of butter and maple syrup.

1 cup buckwheat flour
½ cup whole wheat flour
½ cup cornmeal
½ cup raw wheat germ
½ cup milk powder
2 teaspoons baking powder
1 teaspoon salt
2 tablespoons oil

At Home: Combine ingredients in a ziplock plastic bag.

In Camp: Empty contents of bag into a bowl or pot. Stir in *2–3 cups* of water. Cook pancakes in a hot oiled pan.

Variations: Add raisins or dried bananas, chopped small.

Breads to Make in Camp

Fresh bread in camp after a few days of backpacking is a real treat. Bake extra for lunches or breakfast.

Care must be taken when baking pan breads on a fuel stove, as the heat is fierce and the bread will easily scorch. Using a thick-bottomed pan or a heat diffuser between the pan and the stove and keeping the heat down will prevent this.

If fresh-baked bread in camp is something you enjoy often while backpacking, consider bringing a camp oven along.

We have included two steamed-bread recipes that take a while to cook, but the breads are wonderfully moist and tender.

Corn Bread

================================

makes 1 8-inch pan's worth

Everybody likes corn bread hot from the pan. Serve it with maple syrup for breakfast, smothered in chili for dinner, dripping with butter and honey for dessert, or cold with peanut butter or cheese for lunch. Use the longer cooking time if you are at eight thousand feet or higher.

¾ cup cornmeal
¾ cup whole wheat flour
⅓ cup raw wheat germ
3 tablespoons buttermilk powder
1½ teaspoons baking powder
½ teaspoon baking soda
2 tablespoons honey
¼ cup minus 1 tablespoon oil

At Home: Combine dry ingredients in a ziplock plastic bag. Pour honey and oil into a capped plastic bottle.

In Camp: Add honey and oil with *¾ cup* of water to dry ingredients. Mix to combine. Pour into a greased 8-inch pan, cover, and steam for 30–40 minutes (use the steaming instructions on page 18). The bread will be springy to the touch. Cover again and steam an extra 10 minutes if necessary.

Alternatively, you can use a frying pan with a lid, with a heat diffuser between the pan and the flame. Cook for 20 minutes, then flip the bread over to complete cooking. With this method, corn bread has to be watched carefully, as a thin pan and a fierce flame will burn the bread's bottom before it is cooked.

Variations: Add one of the following: 2 teaspoons cumin; ½ cup fresh-grated Parmesan cheese; 1 teaspoon chili flakes; 2 tablespoons chopped pecans or hazelnuts and 2 tablespoons sunflower or sesame seeds.

Irish Soda Bread

==

makes 1 small loaf

Serve with Spinach Clam Soup (page 126) for a hearty dinner.

¾ cup whole wheat flour
2 tablespoons buttermilk powder
½ teaspoon baking soda
½ teaspoon baking powder

At Home: Combine ingredients in a ziplock plastic bag.

In Camp: Empty contents of bag into a bowl or pot. Add *½ cup* of water and mix well. Place the dough in an oiled, thick-bottomed pan, or use a heat diffuser. Use the stove's lowest heat, turning dough after its bottom has firmed up. Turn it several times. A lid on the pan will make the bread cook a little faster. The bread will take about 20 minutes to cook and will sound hollow when you tap the crust.

Variations: Use half unbleached white, half whole wheat flour; add 1 tablespoon dried mixed herbs; add a handful of dried fruit or raisins; add zest from half a lemon or add ¼ teaspoon caraway seeds.

Whole Wheat Bread

makes 1 loaf or 12 scones

This is a luxury bread for long trips; save leftovers for lunch, if you can stop eating it. The bread will rise as you hike.

1½ cups whole wheat flour
¼ cup raw wheat germ
pinch of salt
1 tablespoon dry yeast
1 tablespoon molasses *or* honey

At Home: In a sturdy, airtight, 1-gallon plastic bag, combine flour, wheat germ, salt, and yeast. Carry molasses or honey in an airtight plastic bottle.

In Camp: Add molasses and *1 cup* of lukewarm water to the bag of flour mixture; mix by stirring or squeezing the mixture in the bag until it is well blended. Twist-tie the bag, leaving plenty of air space for the bread to expand. Place the dough in your pack carefully, or it could be a real mess. Leave it to rise for a few hours to all day. At the end of the day, knead the dough and form it into a round loaf.

There are three methods for baking: Oil or dust with flour a thick-bottomed pan and place the loaf in it. Cover the loaf with a bandana or plastic bag, and let it rise again in the sunshine for 20 minutes. If the sun is down, warm the pan first and let the dough sit in the warm covered pan. Cook over low heat, turning, for about 15–20 minutes, or until bread sounds hollow when you tap the crust.

Cook as individual Drop Scones (page 117) in an oiled pan for 10–15 minutes.

Steam the bread (follow directions on page 18) after letting the dough rise in the steaming bowl for 20 minutes in a warm spot. (To make the dough rise, warm the water and place the bowl in it.) After the dough rises, bring the water to a boil; start timing after it comes to a boil. The bread will take 30 minutes to steam—the top will be springy to the touch. This is by far the most successful method.

Singing Hinnies

■■■■■■■■■■■■■■■■■■■■■■■■■■■■■

makes 4

This is an old country recipe from the British Isles. Its name comes from the sizzling butter, which was thought to be singing.

1 cup unbleached flour *or* whole wheat flour
¼ cup brown rice flour
¼ cup milk powder
1 teaspoon baking powder
3 tablespoons butter
handful of raisins
2 tablespoons extra flour

At Home: Sift together dry ingredients, then mix the butter and dry ingredients together by rubbing the mixture between your thumb and forefinger until the dry ingredients are coated with butter. Package in a ziplock plastic bag with raisins. Package extra flour separately.

In Camp: Empty flour mixture into a bowl or pot. Add ½ *cup* of water, combine well, and pat into four flat disks about ½ inch thick. Dust your hands with a little of the extra flour so you don't get sticky.

Heat a thick-bottomed pan (or use a heat diffuser) over moderate heat, drop in the Hinnies, and cook, turning once, for about 15 minutes. They will cook a little quicker with a lid on. Keep flame low.

Eat well buttered and save extras for lunch.

Rye Batter Bread

==

makes 1 loaf

This bread can be made with many variations to suit your taste buds. The recipe is large enough for dinner and lunch the next day; halve it if you want to reduce cooking time.

2 cups rye flour
1 cup whole wheat flour
pinch of salt
2 teaspoons baking soda
6 tablespoons buttermilk powder
3 tablespoons oil or butter

Flavorings:
2 tablespoons dried onion and 2 teaspoons dried dill
   or 2 teaspoons caraway seed *or* fennel seed
   or 2 teaspoons dried orange peel and 1 teaspoon
     crushed cardamom
   or ½ cup dried raisins and 1 teaspoon cinnamon
   or ½ cup grated Parmesan cheese and 2
     tablespoons dried pepper flakes
1–3 tablespoons molasses, depending on sweetness
   desired

At Home: Package dry ingredients together in a ziplock plastic bag, including your choice of flavorings. Combine oil and molasses in a plastic bottle with a lid.

In Camp: Add *1⅔ cups* of water and the molasses mixture to the dry ingredients and mix to combine. Don't overmix, or you will toughen the dough. Pour into an oiled pan and bake without delay for 20–40 minutes, depending on your cooking method.

    Steam, according to the steaming directions on page 18, for 40 minutes, or until bread is springy to the touch.

Bake in an oiled frying pan using a heat diffuser between the flame and the pan. Flip to bake the other side when the top begins to set, after about 30 minutes.

Bake for about 20 minutes in a stove-top or camp oven. (See Stoves, page 16.)

Drop Scones

————————————————————————

makes 1 dozen

Serve as a bread with dinner and bake extras for lunch. There are many variations, from sweet to savory.

½ cup whole wheat flour
½ cup unbleached white flour
2 tablespoons buttermilk powder
2 teaspoons baking powder
1 tablespoon butter
1 egg (optional)

At Home: Combine dry ingredients, then mix the butter and dry ingredients together by rubbing the mixture between your thumb and forefinger until the dry ingredients are coated with butter. Package in a ziplock plastic bag.

In Camp: Add the egg and ¾–1 *cup* of water–enough to make a thick batter–to the bagged ingredients. Mix well. Drop from a spoon into a slightly greased hot frying pan. When puffed and full of bubbles, turn and brown the other side.

Variations: For sweet scones add ¼ cup dried cranberries with ½ teaspoon lemon or orange zest and 2 tablespoons chopped walnuts; ½ cup dried berries of your choice; or ½ teaspoon mixed spices–cinnamon, nutmeg, etc. For savory scones add 1 teaspoon herbes de Provence and ½ cup Parmesan cheese.

Soups

It's easy and satisfying to package your own soup mixes—you control what goes into them, keep the cost down, and add variety and nutrition. All of these soups are quick and easy to make.

Garlic Broth

This basic and nourishing broth is easy and inexpensive to make. It's fine the way it is or with a little Parmesan cheese sprinkled on top. It's also a good base for soup or stew or for cooking dumplings. Try it with a fresh potato cooked in it, or with rice or lentils.

20–30 garlic cloves, crushed
2 tablespoons parsley flakes
1 teaspoon sage
1 teaspoon thyme
1 whole clove
1 small bay leaf
2 tablespoons olive oil (optional)

At Home: Combine ingredients and package in a ziplock plastic bag.

In Camp: Add the ingredients to *4 cups* of water or stock. Bring to a boil, reduce heat, and simmer, covered, for 15 minutes or longer. Sprinkle on Sesame Salt (page 84).

Herb Vegetable Broth

Use this to simmer dumplings, noodles, or Chinese bean threads, or serve it as a cup of broth on its own.

1 vegetable bouillon cube *or* 1 tablespoon bouillon
    powder
2 tablespoons dried mushrooms, chopped fine
2 tablespoons dried chives
1 tablespoon mixed dried herbs
2 garlic cloves, crushed
4 sun-dried tomatoes, chopped

At Home: Package all ingredients in a ziplock plastic bag.

In Camp: Empty contents of bag into a cook pot and stir in *4 cups* of water. Bring to a boil, cover, and simmer 3–5 minutes.

Variations: Add a fresh grated carrot and/or a chopped onion.

Miso Soup

Miso is worth its weight in gold. It can make a complete meal or be a very good hot broth by itself for quick energy. It's good for breakfast, too.

1 4-by-4-inch piece of kombu (seaweed)
3 tablespoons dried fish flakes *or* handful of iriko
      (small dried fish)
2 tablespoons miso
2 teaspoons tamari
1 teaspoon toasted sesame oil

At Home: Combine kombu and fish flakes in an airtight plastic bag. Combine the miso, tamari, and oil and package separately.

In Camp: Bring *4 cups* of water to a boil. Stir in the kombu mixture and boil for 5 minutes. Stir in the miso mixture, heat thoroughly, and serve.

Variations: Add *1 cup* of noodles at the beginning; drop in Dilly Dumplings (page 146) at the beginning and cook 10 minutes in all; add dried shrimp at the beginning, or canned fish or shrimp at the end.

Garnishes: Sliced lemon; broken pieces of Zwieback (page 49); popcorn; dried chives; Parmesan cheese.

Fish Soup

===

This is a nice change from steamed or fried fish. Use a fillet of fresh fish, or else use canned fish.

6 ounces noodles: spinach, whole wheat, *or* vegetable
1 bay leaf
1 vegetable bouillon cube *or* 1 tablespoon vegetable
    bouillon powder *or* 1 tablespoon mixed dried
    herbs
pinch of black pepper
1 cup fresh fish fillet *or* 1 can tuna or other fish

At Home: Package all ingredients except the fish in a ziplock plastic bag.

In Camp: Bring *4 cups* of water to a boil. Stir in noodle mixture and boil for 5 minutes. Then stir in the fresh filleted fish and cook an additional 5 minutes. If you are using canned fish, stir it in once the noodles are cooked.

Tasty Noodle Soup with Seaweed

serves 4

With this recipe, you can make your own ramen, without the fine-print ingredients. It's good hot or cold.

8 ounces instant Oriental egg noodles (they look like ramen)
½ cup dried sea palm or wakame (or combination)
1 tablespoon dried cilantro *or* dried chives
2 tablespoons crushed garlic
2 tablespoons freshly grated gingerroot
1 tablespoon olive oil
1 tablespoon toasted sesame oil
1 teaspoon honey

At Home: Place noodles and seaweed in separate airtight bags. Put cilantro or chives, garlic, and ginger in another bag. Pack oils and honey in small bottles.

In Camp: Bring a pot of water to boil and add noodles. Boil until done, about 3 minutes. Drain noodles, place in a separate bowl, toss with olive oil, and set aside. While noodles are cooking, soak seaweed for about 5 minutes in a cup, bowl, or small pot. Combine the rest of the ingredients in the pot used to boil the noodles, and add the drained seaweed. Sauté for 3–5 minutes. Add *8 cups* of water and bring to a boil. Remove from heat, add noodles, stir, and serve.

Mushroom Ginger Noodle Soup

serves 4

Shiitake and maitake mushrooms, olive oil, ginger, and garlic are all considered to be beneficial to our bodies. Sit back, sip, and know you are doing something good for yourself while relishing this gourmet soup.

½ ounce dried shiitake and maitake mushrooms
1 tablespoon powdered mushroom *or* mushroom
        paste
2 vegetable bouillon cubes *or* equivalent to make 5
        cups stock
8 ounces fine egg noodles
2 garlic cloves, crushed
1-inch piece gingerroot, grated
1 tablespoon olive oil
1 teaspoon soy sauce

At Home: Package dried mushrooms and mushroom powder in a small bag. Package garlic and ginger in another bag. Carry noodles, bouillon, soy sauce, and olive oil separately. Put all bags and containers in one bag.

In Camp: Cover mushrooms and mushroom powder with 1¼ *cups* of water and let soak for about 30 minutes, depending on thickness of mushrooms.

After about 15 minutes, add bouillon to 5 *cups* of water in a separate pot and bring to a boil. Remove from heat, add noodles, cover, and wrap pot in a towel or blanket. Let sit for 10 minutes; the noodles will cook without further heat.

Drain the mushroom liquid into the noodle mixture, squeezing out the excess juice from the mushrooms. Sauté garlic, grated ginger, and mushrooms for 2 minutes in the olive oil. Add that to the noodle mixture and bring to a boil. Turn off heat, add soy sauce, and stir. Serve immediately.

Partan Bree

- -

serves 2

This mild, milky Scottish soup, light in flavor, is good on those nights when you need something soothing.

½ cup milk powder
¼ cup rolled oats
2 tablespoons dried chives
1 teaspoon parsley flakes
¼ teaspoon salt
¼ teaspoon nutmeg
pepper to taste
2 tablespoons butter (optional)
1 6½-ounce can crab meat with juice

At Home: Package dry ingredients together in a ziplock plastic bag. Carry the butter and crab separately.

In Camp: Place dry ingredients in a cook pot and slowly add *4 cups* of water. Bring to a boil, stirring constantly. Cover, reduce heat, and simmer 5–10 minutes. Remove from heat and stir in the butter and crab, with juice from the can.

Spinach Clam Soup

This tasty soup is high in iron. Serve with Irish Soda Bread (page 113).

½ cup dehydrated spinach
1 tablespoon onion flakes
1 teaspoon parsley flakes
1 teaspoon basil
dash of nutmeg
dash of pepper
1 6½-ounce can clams with juice

At Home: Package the dry ingredients in a ziplock plastic bag. Carry the clams separately.

In Camp: Place the dry ingredients in a cook pot and slowly add *3½ cups* of water. Bring to a boil, stirring constantly. Reduce heat, cover, and simmer for 3 minutes. Remove from heat, stir in clams with juice from can, and heat through. Garnish with Parmesan cheese or chopped almonds.

Minestrone

This classic soup will keep you warm on a chilly day.

½ cup freeze-dried pinto beans, black beans, *or* lentils
4 ounces broken spaghetti
¼ cup grated Parmesan cheese
2 tablespoons tomato powder *or* 1 vegetable bouillon
    cube
2 tablespoons parsley flakes
1 tablespoon dehydrated spinach flakes (optional)
1 tablespoon onion flakes *or* 1 small fresh onion,
    chopped in camp
1 tablespoon celery flakes
1 tablespoon dried bell pepper (optional)
1–2 teaspoons basil
1 teaspoon oregano
½ teaspoon each salt and pepper
1 garlic clove, minced in camp, *or* ¼ teaspoon garlic
    powder

At Home: Package ingredients together in a ziplock
plastic bag.

In Camp: Place ingredients in a cook pot and slowly
add *4 cups* of water. Bring to a boil, stirring constantly. Reduce heat, cover, and simmer 5–10 minutes
or until the spaghetti and beans are tender.

Hot Pot Soup

serves 1 as main course, 2 as first course

This warming, satisfying soup is a meal in itself, but a chunk of bread will round the meal out. The amount of chili you use depends on your closeness to the border!

½ cup finely chopped sun-dried tomatoes
⅓ cup polenta
¼–½ pasilla chili, seeds removed, finely shredded
2 bouillon cubes *or* 1 tablespoon powdered bouillon
2 teaspoons dried onion
1 teaspoon ground cumin
1 tablespoon Mexican oregano
1 teaspoon salt

At Home: Package ingredients together in a ziplock plastic bag.

In Camp: Bring *3 cups* of water to a rolling boil and stir in ingredients. Cover, reduce heat, and simmer for 10 minutes.

Variations: Add a whole garlic clove in camp; smother soup in cheese (Parmesan, cheddar, or jack) and cover for a few seconds for the cheese to melt.

Salsa Soup with Corn Cheese Dumplings

serves 2

Olé!

¼ cup tomato powder
2 tablespoons dried onion
2 tablespoons dried bell pepper
2 garlic cloves, minced at home, *or* ¼ teaspoon garlic
    powder
1–3 teaspoons dried cilantro
1 teaspoon dried oregano
1 teaspoon cumin seeds, ground
½ teaspoon red chili powder
Corn Cheese Dumplings (page 148)

At Home: Combine ingredients (except dumpling ingredients) in a ziplock plastic bag.

In Camp: Empty contents of bag into a cook pot and slowly stir in *4 cups* of water. (For directions on preparing the dumpling batter, see page 148.) Bring to a boil over moderate heat, stirring constantly. Reduce heat to simmer, and drop in the dumpling batter by the spoonful. Cover. Do not peek or lift the lid for 10 minutes. When finished, the dumplings will be puffed and springy to the touch. If necessary, cook 5 minutes more.

If you are making soup without the dumplings, after bringing to a boil, cover the pot and simmer 5–10 minutes.

Spiced Tomato Millet Soup

serves 2

This is an exotic, flavorful soup. Serve it with pocket bread or Potato Cakes (page 61) for a full meal.

⅓ cup millet
1 teaspoon coriander seeds
½ teaspoon fennel seeds
½ teaspoon cardamom seeds
½ teaspoon fenugreek seeds
½ teaspoon turmeric
3 tablespoons tomato powder
2 garlic cloves, minced at home, *or* ½ teaspoon garlic
        powder
pinch of cayenne
salt to taste

At Home: In a dry skillet over moderate heat, toast millet, stirring occasionally. Cool, and crack millet in a blender. Grind all the seeds with a mortar and pestle, coffee grinder, or electric mill. Combine all ingredients in a ziplock plastic bag.

In Camp: In a cook pot, bring *4 cups* of water to a boil. Stir in contents of bag, reduce heat, cover, and simmer 10–15 minutes.

Spicy Hot & Sour Soup

serves 2

This is a delightful, tasty soup. It has an authentic flavor for Chinese-food lovers. Serve it with Oriental Brown Rice Cakes (page 70), Soybean Burgers (page 66), or over a bowl of boiled noodles.

2 tablespoons white, rice, *or* cider vinegar
2 tablespoons tamari
2 tablespoons rice wine *or* cooking sherry
1 tablespoon cornstarch *or* arrowroot powder
2 teaspoons toasted sesame oil
1 vegetable bouillon cube *or* 1 tablespoon vegetable
     bouillon powder
1 teaspoon freshly grated gingerroot
6 Chinese black mushrooms, minced
1–2 eggs (optional)

At Home: Combine ingredients except mushrooms and eggs in a plastic bottle with a lid. Remove woody stems from mushrooms and finely chop the caps. Package in a ziplock plastic bag. Carry the eggs whole in an egg container.

In Camp: In a cook pot, cover mushrooms with water and soak for 30 minutes. Stir in the bottled ingredients and add *4 cups* of water. Bring soup to a boil over moderate heat, cover, reduce heat, and cook 3–5 minutes, stirring occasionally. In a bowl, beat eggs well with a fork. Give the soup a stir, and pour in the eggs as the soup bubbles. Stir well. This will make egg "threads." Serve immediately.

Five-Grain Soup

serves 2

This is a filling, creamy soup, and quick cooking. It's very good for a rainy-day lunch in the tent. Serve it with cheese or peanut butter and crackers. It's good with Journey Cakes (page 60), too.

3 tablespoons rolled oats
2 tablespoons dehydrated diced potato *or* 1 baked potato, chopped small
1 tablespoon whole wheat flour
1 tablespoon barley flour
1 tablespoon millet flour
1 tablespoon rye flour
1 tablespoon nutritional yeast (optional)
1 tablespoon milk powder
1 tablespoon dehydrated carrots
1 tablespoon onion flakes
1 teaspoon parsley flakes
½ teaspoon salt
dash of garlic granules *or* 1 fresh clove garlic, chopped at home

At Home: Package ingredients in a ziplock plastic bag.

In Camp: Empty ingredients into a cook pot and slowly add *4 cups* of water. Bring to a boil, stirring constantly. Cover, reduce heat, and simmer for 5–10 minutes.

Spinach Cheese Soup

==

This recipe serves two for lunch or before a main course for dinner. Doubled, it serves two for dinner along with bread or Journey Cakes (page 60).

½ cup milk powder
2 tablespoons flour
2 tablespoons spinach flakes
1 tablespoon onion flakes
1 tablespoon parsley flakes (optional)
¼ teaspoon salt
pinch of cayenne
1 garlic clove, crushed at home, *or* ⅛ teaspoon garlic
    granules
handful of toasted chopped almonds (optional)
½ cup grated or diced cheddar cheese *or* 1 cup grated
    Parmesan cheese
2 tablespoons vermouth (optional)

At Home: Combine dry ingredients in a ziplock plastic bag. Package cheese separately. Carry vermouth in a plastic bottle.

In Camp: Put dry ingredients in a cook pot, and slowly add *3 cups* of water. Bring to a boil, stirring constantly. Cover, reduce heat, and simmer for 3–5 minutes. Remove pot from heat, and stir in the cheese and vermouth.

Potato Cheese Soup

For those nights when you want a thick, filling soup, use this version of an Old World classic recipe.

½ cup dehydrated potato pieces *or* 1 unpeeled baked
　　　potato, chopped small
½ cup milk powder
2 tablespoons rolled oats
2 tablespoons whole wheat flour
1 tablespoon onion flakes
1 tablespoon raw wheat germ
1 garlic clove, minced at home, *or* ¼ teaspoon garlic
　　　powder
1 teaspoon parsley flakes
1 teaspoon dill weed (optional)
½ teaspoon salt
dash each of pepper and nutmeg
½ pound cheddar cheese, cut in chunks, *or* ¼ pound
　　　Parmesan cheese, grated

At Home: Combine dry ingredients in a ziplock plastic bag. Package cheese separately.

In Camp: Empty dry ingredients into a cook pot and slowly add *4 cups* of water. Bring to a boil, stirring constantly. Cover, reduce heat, and simmer for 3–5 minutes. Remove from heat and stir in cheese.

Minted Cream of Pea Soup

serves 2

This is a delicate soup with a fresh pea flavor, perfumed with mint. Serve it as a light snack with steamed Corn Bread (page 112) or crackers and cheese.

½ cup milk powder
2 ounces freeze-dried peas
3 tablespoons flour
2 tablespoons dried chives
1 tablespoon dried mint
¼ teaspoon nutmeg
2 garlic cloves, minced at home, *or* ½ teaspoon garlic
    powder
salt and pepper to taste

At Home: Combine ingredients in a ziplock plastic bag.

In Camp: Empty contents of bag into a cook pot. Slowly stir in *4 cups* of water. Bring to a boil, cover, reduce heat, and simmer for 3–5 minutes. Stir occasionally to prevent sticking.

Cream of Tomato Soup

serves 2

This is a light soup for lunch or before dinner. For a complete meal, add a can of seafood or some cubed cheese. Serve with steamed Corn Bread (page 112), Potato Cakes (page 61), or Corn Crackers (page 51).

½ cup milk powder
¼ cup tomato powder
3 tablespoons flour
1 tablespoon dried chives
2 teaspoons basil
2 garlic cloves, minced at home, *or* ½ teaspoon garlic powder
4 sun-dried tomatoes, chopped
pinch of cayenne
½ teaspoon salt

At Home: Package ingredients in a ziplock plastic bag.

In Camp: Empty the contents of the bag into a cook pot. Slowly stir in *4 cups* of water. Stir over moderate heat, and bring to a boil. Cover, reduce heat, and simmer, stirring occasionally, for 3–5 minutes.

Variations: Add 1 teaspoon dried orange rind; 1 tablespoon mint or mixed herbs; or 1 tablespoon mild curry powder and 6 dried apple rings, chopped.

Cream of Celery Soup

serves 2

The delicate flavor of celery comes through in this thick, creamy soup. It's good with Journey Cakes (page 60) or herbed Drop Scones (page 117).

½ cup mashed potato powder *or* 3 tablespoons flour
½ cup milk powder
4 tablespoons celery flakes
1 tablespoon onion flakes
1 garlic clove, crushed at home, *or* ¼ teaspoon garlic
    powder
½ teaspoon salt
¼ teaspoon black pepper
pinch of nutmeg
½ cup grated Parmesan cheese (optional)

At Home: Combine dry ingredients in a ziplock plastic bag. Package cheese separately.

In Camp: Empty contents of bag into a cook pot. Slowly stir in *4 cups* of water. Bring to a boil over moderate heat, stirring frequently. Reduce heat, cover, and simmer 3–5 minutes. Stir in Parmesan cheese and serve.

Cream of Mushroom Soup

This is a good winter soup. It has a strong mushroom flavor and is thick and creamy.

⅓ cup dried mushrooms, chopped fine
⅓ cup milk powder
2 tablespoons flour
2 teaspoons nutritional yeast (optional)
2 teaspoons raw wheat germ
1 tablespoon onion flakes
1 teaspoon parsley flakes
½ teaspoon salt
1 clove garlic, minced at home, *or* ¼ teaspoon garlic
    powder
dash of nutmeg
dash of pepper

At Home: Package ingredients in a ziplock plastic bag.

In Camp: Empty contents of bag into a cook pot. Slowly add *4 cups* of water. Bring to a boil, stirring constantly. Reduce heat, cover, and simmer for 5–10 minutes.

Nut Butter Soup

Try this creamy soup with Corn Bread (page 112).

½ cup milk powder
2 tablespoons whole wheat flour
1 tablespoon onion flakes
½ teaspoon salt
¼ teaspoon celery seed
¼ teaspoon pepper
1 bay leaf
½ cup peanut, almond, *or* cashew butter
2 tablespoons grated Parmesan cheese (optional)

At Home: Combine dry ingredients in a ziplock plastic bag. Carry nut butter and cheese separately.

In Camp: Place dry ingredients in a cook pot, and slowly add *4 cups* of water. Bring to a boil, stirring constantly. Cover, reduce heat, and simmer for 5 minutes. Remove from heat, and stir in nut butter and cheese.

Clam Chowder

This creamy chowder is always satisfying.

½ cup dehydrated diced potato *or* 1 baked unpeeled
    potato, chopped very small in camp
¼ cup milk powder
2 tablespoons flour
1 tablespoon celery flakes
1 teaspoon dill weed
¼ teaspoon salt
¼ teaspoon black pepper *or* ⅛ teaspoon Asian chili
    flakes
1 garlic clove, minced at home, *or* ¼ teaspoon garlic
    powder
1 tablespoon chicken or vegetable bouillon powder
    (optional)
1 6½-ounce can minced clams, with juice

At Home: Package dry ingredients in a ziplock plastic
bag. Carry clams (and baked potato, if using one)
separately.

In Camp: Empty contents of bag into a cook pot, and
slowly add *4 cups* of water. Bring to a boil, stirring
constantly. Cover, reduce heat, and simmer for 3–5
minutes. Stir in the clams with their juice.

Corn Chowder

This is a thick, creamy chowder. It's high in protein and a special treat with the added crab.

½ cup dehydrated corn
½ cup freeze-dried potatoes *or* 1 unpeeled baked
        potato, cut in small pieces in camp
2 tablespoons cornmeal
2 tablespoons whole wheat flour
2 tablespoons milk powder
1 teaspoon parsley flakes
1 tablespoon onion flakes
1 teaspoon celery flakes
1 teaspoon dill, thyme, *or* savory
½ teaspoon salt
½ teaspoon paprika
dash of pepper
1 tablespoon butter
1 6½-ounce can crab meat and juice (optional)

At Home: Combine all ingredients, except crab (and baked potato, if using one), in a ziplock plastic bag.

In Camp: Empty contents of bag into a cook pot. Slowly stir in 4½ *cups* of water. Bring to a boil over moderate heat, stirring. Reduce heat and simmer, covered, for 10 minutes. Add crab with juice from can, heat through, and serve.

Patties & Dumplings

A bowl of soup topped with dumplings or accompanied by a patty, made fresh in camp, makes a satisfying, complete meal. Patties are also good smothered with a sauce, spread, or gravy.

Meal Cakes

These cakes will form a brown crust on the outside, and the inside will slightly steam. They are very satisfying in cold weather for breakfast. Or eat them cold, later in the day, with peanut butter and honey or a dessert topping.

½ cup sunflower seeds, ground
½ cup almonds, ground
½ cup whole wheat flour
½ cup corn grits
¼ teaspoon salt

At Home: Grind the seeds and nuts in a blender, food processor, or coffee grinder. Combine all ingredients in a ziplock plastic bag.

In Camp: Place ingredients in a bowl. Add *1 cup* of hot water, stir, and let stand for 15 minutes or so. Take a heaping tablespoon, form a ball (the dough will be moist), and pat into a pancake shape about ½ inch thick. Cook in a lightly greased pan for 10–15 minutes. Serve with butter and honey or Date Walnut Topping (page 237).

Variation: For a dinner entrée add 1 medium onion, chopped fine in camp, or 1 tablespoon onion flakes; 1 teaspoon savory or your favorite herb; and another 1/4 teaspoon salt.

Cook as above. Serve with tamari or Nut Butter Sauce (page 165).

Sesame Seed Patties

serves 2

These tasty, crunchy patties are good with a sauce, gravy, hot mustard, or just tamari.

1 cup sesame seeds ground in a grinder or blender
¼ cup soy flour
¼ cup raw wheat germ
1 teaspoon onion flakes
1 teaspoon parsley flakes
1 teaspoon sage
¼ teaspoon garlic granules *or* ½ teaspoon garlic
    powder
½ teaspoon celery seeds
¼ teaspoon salt
oil for sautéing

At Home: Combine dry ingredients in a ziplock plastic bag. Carry the oil searately.

In Camp: Add ⅓ *cup* of water to the mixture in the bag and squeeze the bag to mix well. Form into six patties 1½ inches in diameter and ½ inch thick and sauté about 7 minutes per side.

Sunflower Seed Patties

serves 2

These have a mild sunflower seed flavor. They are very good with Curry Sauce (page 164) or Mushroom Sauce (page 163).

1 cup raw sunflower seeds, ground
2 tablespoons whole wheat flour
1 teaspoon celery flakes
1 teaspoon parsley flakes
½ teaspoon chervil
¼ teaspoon salt
¼ teaspoon savory
⅛ teaspoon garlic granules (optional)
oil for sautéing

At Home: Combine dry ingredients in a ziplock plastic bag. Carry the oil separately.

In Camp: Leave the ingredients in the plastic bag and add 2–3 *tablespoons* of water. Squeeze the mixture in the bag until the ingredients are mixed. Let rest for a few minutes. Form into four small patties and sauté in a little oil about 5–7 minutes per side.

Dilly Dumplings

serves 2 as main course, 4 as side dish

This recipe turns leftover fish into a new filling meal. Cook in Garlic Broth (page 119) or Herb Vegetable Broth (page 120). The dumplings may also be fried as patties.

½ cup raw wheat germ
½ cup brown rice flour
2 teaspoons dill weed
1 teaspoon baking powder
¼ teaspoon salt (optional)
1 cup cooked leftover fish *or* 1 6½-ounce can fish
2 teaspoons oil (optional)

At Home: Place dry ingredients in a ziplock plastic bag. Carry the fish and oil separately.

In Camp: Flake the leftover fish or drain the can of fish and combine in a bowl with dry ingredients, oil, and ½ cup of water. Drop by the spoonful into hot broth and cook, tightly covered, for 10 minutes before checking. The dumplings should be puffed and springy to the touch. Cover and cook for 5 minutes more if necessary.

Herb or Spice Dumplings

▄▄▄▄▄▄▄▄▄▄▄▄▄▄▄▄▄▄▄▄▄▄▄▄▄▄▄▄▄▄▄▄▄▄

serves 2 as main course, 4 as side dish

Plop the herb dumplings into a soup or broth, or the spicy ones into Stewed Fruit Sauce (page 167). Don't peek.

1 cup whole wheat flour
4 tablespoons milk powder
2 tablespoons rolled oats
2 teaspoons baking powder
¼ teaspoon salt
2 tablespoons butter
For Herb Dumplings, add 2 teaspoons dried mixed herbs.
For Spice Dumplings, add 1 teaspoon mixed spices (cinnamon, nutmeg, cloves, allspice, cardamom) and ¼ cup chopped walnuts or pecans.

At Home: Combine dry ingredients and cut in the butter. Pack in a ziplock plastic bag.

In Camp: Add *½ cup* water to the bagged ingredients and squeeze the mixture in the bag to mix. Drop by the spoonful into bubbling soup or broth. Cover tightly and keep at a steady simmer. Check after 10 minutes. The dumplings should be puffed and springy to the touch. Cover and cook for 5 minutes more if necessary.

Corn Cheese Dumplings

serves 2 as main course, 4 as side dish

These dumplings are great cooked in Salsa Soup (page 129).

½ cup cornmeal
½ cup flour
¼ cup milk powder
2 teaspoons baking powder
½ teaspoon cumin
3 tablespoons grated Parmesan cheese

At Home: Combine all ingredients in a ziplock plastic bag.

In Camp: Add ½ *cup* of water to the bag of ingredients and squeeze the mixture in the bag to mix. Drop by the spoonful into bubbling soup or broth. Cover tightly and keep at a steady simmer. Check after 10 minutes. The dumplings should be puffed and springy to the touch. Cover and cook for 5 minutes more if necessary.

Brown Rice Dumplings

serves 2 as main course, 4 as side dish

These have a mild, plain flavor. They are good in spicy soups or stews.

¼ cup brown rice flour
¾ cup flour
¼ cup raw wheat germ
2 tablespoons milk powder
2 teaspoons baking powder
¼ teaspoon salt
2 tablespoons butter
1 egg (essential)

At Home: Combine dry ingredients, and then rub in the butter with your fingertips. Package in a ziplock plastic bag. Carry egg separately in an egg container.

In Camp: Add ½ *cup* of water and the egg to the bag of dry ingredients; mix well. Drop by the spoonful into bubbling soup. Cover tightly and simmer without peeking for 10 minutes. The dumplings should be puffed and tender. Cover and cook for 5 minutes more if necessary.

Variations: Add 1 tablespoon paprika; 1 tablespoon curry powder; 1 tablespoon dried herbs; or 1 tablespoon mixed spices (cinnamon, nutmeg, and so on).

Sauces & Dips

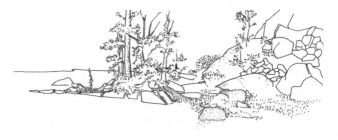

Sauces turn pasta, grains, or patties into something special. Nourishing and inexpensive, they add variety in taste and are simple to make. Dips are great eaten with lunches and snacks.

Tomato Curry Sauce

makes approximately 2½ cups

This turns out thick, like a chowder. It's easy and quick to make, even in your tent on a snowy eve. It's good served over noodles or grains.

¼ cup tomato powder
5 teaspoons mild curry powder
1 tablespoon parsley flakes
½ teaspoon cumin seeds, crushed
½ teaspoon coriander seeds, crushed
½ teaspoon ginger
½ teaspoon salt
½ teaspoon tarragon (optional)
1 tablespoon onion flakes
2 cloves garlic, minced, *or* ¼ teaspoon garlic granules
        or ½ teaspoon garlic powder
2 teaspoons tamari

At Home: Combine all ingredients, including tamari, in a ziplock plastic bag.

In Camp: Place contents of bag in a cook pot. Stirring constantly, add *2 cups* of water. Bring to a boil, reduce heat, cover, and simmer for 5–10 minutes.

Marinara Sauce

makes 3½–4 cups

This is our spaghetti sauce, and we also use it over grains and patties. It tastes like fresh homemade sauce.

½ cup tomato powder
¼ cup dried mushrooms, minced
¼ cup dried bell pepper (optional)
3 tablespoons tomato flakes *or* 4–6 sun-dried
    tomatoes, chopped
1 tablespoon onion flakes
1 tablespoon parsley flakes
1 tablespoon oregano
1 tablespoon basil
½ teaspoon salt
2 garlic cloves, minced at home, *or* ¼ teaspoon garlic
    granules *or* ½ teaspoon garlic powder
1 6½-ounce can crab, clams, *or* shrimp with juice *or*
    ½ cup freeze-dried shrimp (optional)

At Home: Combine dry ingredients in a ziplock plastic bag. Carry seafood separately.

In Camp: Place contents of bag in a cook pot and slowly stir in *3 cups* of water. Bring to a boil, reduce heat, cover, and simmer for 5 minutes. Remove from heat and stir in seafood with juice from can.

Variations: Use 1 small can bonito or mackerel or 1 cup freshly cooked flaked fish instead of the seafood listed.

Chili Sauce

makes approximately 3½ cups

Serve this sauce over grains, noodles, polenta, or Journey Cakes (page 60).

¼ cup tomato powder
1 tablespoon onion flakes
1 tablespoon whole wheat flour *or* masa *or* corn flour
1 teaspoon chili powder
2 teaspoons oregano
1 teaspoon ground cumin
1 teaspoon parsley flakes
½ teaspoon salt
2 cloves garlic, minced, *or* ¼ teaspoon garlic granules
    or ½ teaspoon garlic powder
1 6½-ounce can shrimp (optional)

At Home: Combine dry ingredients in a ziplock plastic bag. Carry shrimp separately.

In Camp: Empty contents of bag into a cook pot. Slowly stir in *3 cups* of water. Bring to a boil, reduce heat, cover, and simmer for 5 minutes. Add shrimp with juice from can and heat through.

Sweet & Sour Sauce

makes 1 cup

Pour this over noodles or rice, or use it as a sauce with fish.

1 ring dried pineapple, chopped fine
1 tablespoon dried bell pepper
1 tablespoon celery flakes
¼ teaspoon garlic granules
2–3 tablespoons red wine vinegar
¼-inch-thick slice fresh gingerroot, chopped fine
1 teaspoon tamari
1 tablespoon honey
1 teaspoon cornstarch

At Home: Package the dried pineapple, vegetables, and garlic in a ziplock plastic bag. In a plastic bottle, combine vinegar, ginger, tamari, honey, and cornstarch. Place bottle in a ziplock plastic bag to avoid spills.

In Camp: Empty both packages into a cook pot. Slowly add ¾ *cup* of water. Bring to a boil, stirring constantly. Reduce heat, cover, and simmer for 2–3 minutes.

Hot & Sour Miso Sauce with Chinese Mushrooms

makes 2 cups

This sauce adds an Asian flavor to Journey Cakes (page 60) or patties; or pour it over noodles or rice.

8 Chinese black mushrooms, caps only, finely
    chopped
1 tablespoon toasted sesame seeds
1 tablespoon cornstarch
½ cup miso
1 tablespoon tamari
2 tablespoons distilled white vinegar
1–2 tablespoons honey
1 tablespoon toasted sesame oil
3 garlic cloves, minced, *or* ½ teaspoon garlic granules,
    or ¾ teaspoon garlic powder
3 25¢-size pieces fresh gingerroot, chopped
1 tablespoon dried onion flakes (optional)
1 tablespoon chili paste *or* ½–1 tablespoon dried red
    chili flakes (optional)

At Home: Package mushrooms and sesame seeds in two separate ziplock plastic bags. Combine remaining ingredients in a plastic bottle. Place the bottle in a ziplock plastic bag to prevent spills.

In Camp: Soak mushrooms in *½ cup* of water for 15–30 minutes. Pour miso mixture into a cook pot and slowly add *1¼ cups* of water and the mushrooms with their soaking liquid. Bring to a boil, stirring constantly. Cover, reduce heat, and simmer for 3–5 minutes. Add toasted sesame seeds.

Tahini Orange Sauce

makes approximately 2 cups

This sauce has the flavor of country gravy. Serve it over whole-grain pastas, Carrot Cakes (page 64), patties, or cooked potatoes.

½ cup sesame tahini
2 tablespoons whole wheat flour
1 tablespoon tamari
1 teaspoon grated orange rind
1 teaspoon honey
1 garlic clove, crushed in camp

At Home: Combine ingredients, except garlic, in a ziplock plastic bag.

In Camp: Put the tahini mixture in a cook pot and place over moderate heat. Slowly stir in the crushed garlic and 1¼ *cups* of water and bring to a boil, stirring constantly. Reduce heat, cover, and simmer for 2–3 minutes.

Spicy Peanut Sauce

makes 1¾ cups

Choose your favorite pasta or noodle and turn your camp into a four-star restaurant!

½ cup creamy or chunky peanut butter
2 tablespoons tamari
4 teaspoons crushed garlic
3 tablespoons apple cider vinegar
2 teaspoons brown sugar
¾ teaspoon dried crushed red pepper
¼ cup chopped fresh cilantro (will remain fresh for at
    least 1–2 days unrefrigerated: the vinegar acts as
    a preservative) *or* 1 tablespoon dried cilantro
salt and pepper to taste

At Home: Combine ingredients in a plastic lidded container. Put in a ziplock bag to protect pack from any leakage.

In Camp: Empty ingredients into a bowl. Slowly stir in ½ *cup* of hot water. Toss through freshly boiled pasta, noodles, or rice.

Variation: Omit cilantro and add 1 tablespoon dried chives or 1 tablespoon freshly grated gingerroot.

Miso Mustard Sauce

makes 1½ cups

This is a hearty sauce, good over Journey Cakes (page 60).

2 tablespoons whole wheat flour
1 tablespoon miso
1 tablespoon Dijon mustard
1 garlic clove, crushed at home, *or* ⅛ teaspoon garlic
    granules *or* ¼ teaspoon garlic powder
¼ teaspoon grated orange peel
dash of honey

At Home: Combine ingredients in a lidded plastic container.

In Camp: Put the miso mixture in a cook pot and gradually stir in *1 cup* of water. Bring to a boil over moderate heat. Reduce heat, cover, and simmer for 2–3 minutes.

Variations: Grate a ½-inch piece of fresh gingerroot instead of orange peel; make a wasabi sauce by replacing the mustard with 1 teaspoon wasabi powder.

Basic White Sauce

makes 1 cup

This is a versatile sauce that, with the addition of herbs, spices, and cheeses, can turn plain grains or pasta into something delicious.

2 tablespoons flour
½ cup milk powder
½ teaspoon dry mustard
salt, pepper, and nutmeg to taste

At Home: Combine ingredients in a ziplock plastic bag.

In Camp: Place ingredients in a cook pot and slowly stir in *1 cup* of water. Cook over moderate heat, stirring until sauce boils and thickens. Cover and simmer for 3–5 minutes to cook the flour.

Variations: To make a cheese sauce, add ½–1 cup grated cheddar cheese or ½ cup grated Parmesan cheese. To make a clam sauce for pasta, add 2 crushed garlic cloves, 1 tablespoon dried basil, 1 tablespoon dried oregano, and a 6½-ounce can clams and their juice. To make a curry sauce, add 1–2 tablespoons curry powder and a handful of raisins.

Cheese Sauce

makes approximately 2 cups

This is a very quick, very creamy sauce.

½ cup milk powder
2 tablespoons flour
1 garlic clove, minced at home, *or* ⅛ teaspoon garlic
        granules *or* ¼ teaspoon garlic powder
1 teaspoon parsley flakes
½ teaspoon dry mustard
dash of cayenne
¼ pound Monterey Jack *or* Parmesan cheese, grated

At Home: Combine all ingredients, except cheese, in a ziplock plastic bag. Carry the cheese separately.

In Camp: Place dry ingredients in a cook pot and slowly stir in 1¾ *cups* of water. Bring to a boil over moderate heat, stirring constantly. Cover, reduce heat, and simmer 2–3 minutes. Remove from heat and stir in cheese.

Tuna Sauce

makes approximately 2½ cups

This recipe is for one of those nights when you counted on fresh fish all day, but for some reason they just weren't biting. You can serve four with one can of tuna by doubling everything else.

¼ cup milk powder
2 tablespoons flour
1 tablespoon parsley flakes
1 garlic clove, minced at home, *or* ¼ teaspoon garlic powder *or* ⅛ teaspoon garlic granules
½ teaspoon dill weed
dash of cayenne *or* black pepper
1 6½-ounce can albacore tuna in oil

At Home: Combine ingredients in a ziplock plastic bag. Carry tuna separately.

In Camp: Combine all ingredients, including tuna with its oil, in a cook pot and stir in *1 cup* of water. Bring to a boil over moderate heat and simmer for 2–3 minutes to cook the flour. Serve hot over grains, noodles, patties, or even broken pieces of bread or toast.

Red Chili Barbecue Sauce

makes 1½ cups

Barbecue flavor without the barbecue! Here's a great all-purpose, richly flavored sauce to spice up rice, noodles—or, if you got lucky, fish.

4 dried pasilla chilies
2 tablespoons olive oil
½ cup tomato puree *or* ¼ cup tomato paste
3 tablespoons soy sauce
2 tablespoons balsamic vinegar
1 tablespoon brown sugar *or* honey
3 garlic cloves, crushed
1 teaspoon ground cumin
1 teaspoon dried oregano
½ teaspoon kosher *or* sea salt
¼ teaspoon freshly ground black pepper

At Home: Remove stems from chilies and cut into 2-inch chunks. Remove most of the seeds if you do not want it too spicy. Pasilla is mild and sweet. In a small skillet, heat the oil and toss the chilies until fragrant, 1–2 minutes. Transfer to a small bowl and submerge in ½–¾ *cup* hot water. Keep chilies submerged with a small plate. Let stand for 30 minutes. Pour chilies and soaking water into a blender or food processor; add the rest of the ingredients and process until smooth. Pour into a leakproof plastic bottle.

In Camp: Pour this flavorful sauce over cooked rice or noodles, or dip freshly cooked fish or Journey Cakes (page 60) in it. Allow about ¼ cup per person per meal.

Mushroom Sauce

makes 1 cup

This is a thick, rich sauce with a mushroom flavor.

⅓ cup dried mushrooms, minced
2 tablespoons whole wheat flour
2 tablespoons milk powder
1 tablespoon dried chopped chives
1 tablespoon vegetable bouillon powder *or* 1
    vegetable bouillon cube
1 teaspoon parsley flakes
1 garlic clove, minced in camp, *or* ⅛ teaspoon garlic
    granules
dash of pepper

At Home: Combine all ingredients in a ziplock plastic bag.

In Camp: Place ingredients in a cook pot. Slowly stir in 1¼ *cups* of water. Bring to a boil, reduce heat, cover, and simmer for 3–5 minutes. Remove from heat and let stand for 5 minutes.

Curry Sauce

============================

makes 1 cup

Bring some spice to your camp with curry sauce over rice.

2 tablespoons milk powder
2 tablespoons flour
1 teaspoon onion flakes
1 garlic clove, minced at home, *or* ⅛ teaspoon garlic
    granules *or* ¼ teaspoon garlic powder
1 teaspoon parsley flakes
1 teaspoon curry powder
¼ teaspoon salt

At Home: Combine all ingredients in an airtight plastic bag.

In Camp: Empty contents of bag into a cook pot. Slowly stir in *1 cup* of water. Bring to a boil, reduce heat, cover, and simmer for 2–3 minutes.

Garlic Sauce

makes 1½ cups

This should be made with fresh garlic.

3-4 garlic cloves, crushed at home
2 tablespoons flour
1 tablespoon vegetable bouillon powder *or* 1
        vegetable bouillon cube
¼ teaspoon black pepper
pinch of cayenne

At Home: Combine ingredients in a ziplock plastic bag.

In Camp: Place ingredients in a cook pot. Slowly stir in *1 cup* of water. Bring to a boil, stirring constantly. Reduce heat, cover, and simmer for 3-5 minutes.

Nut Butter Sauce

makes 1½ cups

Pour this nutty sauce over rice or pasta.

½ cup nut butter of your choice
1 tablespoon whole wheat flour
pinch of garlic granules
dash of cayenne
1 teaspoon tamari

At Home: Combine ingredients in a ziplock plastic bag.

In Camp: Place nut butter mixture in a cook pot and stir in *1 cup* of water. Bring to a boil, reduce heat, cover, and simmer for 3-5 minutes.

Cashew Sauce

makes approximately 3 cups

This is a mild sauce. It's simple to make and adds protein to the meal.

¾ cup raw cashews, ground fine
2 tablespoons arrowroot powder *or* cornstarch
1 teaspoon parsley flakes
1 teaspoon onion powder *or* onion flakes
½ teaspoon celery flakes
⅛ teaspoon celery seeds
1 teaspoon tamari

At Home: Grind cashews in a blender, coffee grinder, or electric mill. Combine all ingredients in a ziplock plastic bag.

In Camp: Put ingredients in a cook pot. Slowly stir in 2½–3 *cups* of water and cook over medium heat, stirring until thick. Serve hot.

Sauces & Dips

Stewed Fruit Sauce

Eaten alone, this is a light breakfast. It can be made heartier served with Drop Scones (page 117) and peanut butter. Or add some spices and serve for dessert, hot or cold. Stewed Fruit Sauce is good over granola, pancakes, corn bread, grains, hot cereal, and Meal Cakes (page 143).

In Camp: Soak *2 cups* of any combination of unsulfured dried fruit overnight in enough water to reach 1 inch above the fruit. In the morning, simmer, covered, over low heat for 5–10 minutes. Use a heat diffuser if necessary to prevent sticking.

Variations: Add 1 teaspoon lemon or orange zest, 1 teaspoon cinnamon, and/or ¼ teaspoon ground cloves.

For Dried Fruit Jam: Barely cover the fruit with water and soak for 10 minutes. Add 1 tablespoon honey per cup of fruit. Simmer until thick, stirring occasionally. Try apricots and dates together.

For Stewed Fruit Soup with Dumplings: Use more water as needed to make a broth. Bring to a boil. Plop Spice Dumplings (page 147) into the bubbling fruit and then follow instructions on page 147.

Raisin Sauce for Pancakes

makes 2¼ cups

This sweet sauce is a breakfast treat.

¾ cup mixed currants, golden raisins, raisins, and
    dates
1 tablespoon cornstarch
honey to taste
1 teaspoon cinnamon
¼ teaspoon nutmeg
pinch of ground cloves

At Home: Combine ingredients in a ziplock plastic bag.

In Camp: Place ingredients in a cook pot. Slowly add
1½ *cups* of water. Cook over moderate heat, stirring
until mixture boils and thickens. Serve over pancakes
or puddings.

Variations: Add 1 teaspoon citrus zest or any dried
fruit; use maple sugar instead of honey; omit the
listed spices and add 1 tablespoon ground ginger.

Honey Syrup

This syrup can be made at home or in camp. It's very simple to make, and warmed up before serving it really makes pancakes seem luxurious.

1 cup honey
1 teaspoon vanilla

Warm the honey, add *1 tablespoon* water and the vanilla, and stir well. Cook over low heat until honey is syrupy. If you make it at home, put it in a squeeze bottle and carry it ready to pour. Reheat it in camp, if you like, by submerging the bottle in hot water while the pancakes cook.

All Dal-ed Up Dip

Masoor dal is a hulled salmon-colored split pea that is sometimes labeled "red lentils" in natural food stores. These tasty legumes are a staple in India and the Middle East. Try this dip with pita bread or fried tortillas. It's also delicious made into a Burrito (page 209) with roasted red pepper and aged cheddar cheese.

1 cup masoor dal
1 teaspoon salt
2 garlic cloves, crushed at home
2 teaspoons freshly grated gingerroot *or* 1 teaspoon
    powdered ginger
1 teaspoon cumin seeds
1 teaspoon coriander seeds, ground
1 teaspoon Asian chili flakes
2 tablespoons olive oil

At Home: Package dal and salt in one plastic ziplock bag and the spices in another. Carry olive oil in a plastic bottle.

In Camp: Bring *3 cups* water to a boil. Add dal, reduce heat to low, and cover, leaving lid ajar to prevent boil-over. Cook 20–30 minutes, then remove from heat and set aside. Sauté spices in oil for 1 minute. Stir in dal and let sit a minute to marry flavors.

One-Pot Luck

These simple meals can be made in one pot. All of the ingredients are usually combined in one bag, are put in a pot of water in camp, and take up to 15 or 20 minutes to cook. They are wholesome, complete meals—satisfying after a day of play in the elements.

Couscous Pilafs

The secret of those expensive prepackaged meals is revealed! Couscous is a pasta product that cooks with just the addition of boiling water. Prepackaging all the flavorings at home makes an instant meal in camp. If you increase the boiling water by ½ cup, bulgur wheat is interchangeable with the couscous; it also requires 15–20 minutes more soaking time.

Moroccan Couscous

serves 2

This is a great side dish or, for a complete meal, serve it with cheese and pocket bread.

⅔ cup couscous
2 tablespoons dried chives
2 teaspoons curry powder
1 tablespoon bouillon powder
3 garlic cloves, minced at home
6–8 sun-dried tomatoes, diced
handful of pistachios *or* pine nuts (optional)

At Home: Combine ingredients in a ziplock plastic bag.

In Camp: Empty contents of bag into a serving bowl or cook pot. Stir in *1 cup* of boiling water. Cover and let the couscous sit undisturbed for 10 minutes. Fluff with a fork.

Taste of India

This couscous dish is sweet and spiced.

⅔ cup couscous
2 teaspoons curry powder
¼ teaspoon whole cardamom seeds, husks removed
1 teaspoon salt
¼ cup currants *or* raisins
2 tablespoons pine nuts

At Home: Combine ingredients in a ziplock plastic bag.

In Camp: Empty contents of bag into a serving bowl or cook pot. Stir in *1 cup* of boiling water. Mix well. Cover and let the couscous sit undisturbed for 10 minutes. Fluff with a fork.

Taste of the Sun

Savor the sun-dried tomatoes in this dish.

⅔ cup couscous
½ cup sun-dried tomatoes, finely chopped
2 teaspoons dried basil
1 tablespoon bouillon powder
1 teaspoon salt
2 tablespoons pine nuts

At Home: Combine ingredients in a ziplock plastic bag.

In Camp: Empty contents of bag into a serving bowl and stir in *1 cup* of boiling water. Mix well. Cover and let sit undisturbed for 10 minutes. Fluff with a fork.

Taste of the Forest

serves 2

The mushrooms and herbs create an earthy flavor.

⅔ cup couscous
½ cup dried mushrooms, finely chopped
1 tablespoon bouillon powder
½–1 teaspoon herbes de Provence
1 teaspoon salt
½ teaspoon fresh cracked pepper

At Home: Combine ingredients in a ziplock plastic bag.

In Camp: Empty contents of bag into a serving bowl or cook pot. Stir in *1½ cups* of boiling water. Mix well. Cover and let the couscous sit undisturbed for 10 minutes. Fluff with a fork.

Taste of Santa Fe

Sit down to a sunset meal and enjoy the pungent flavor of the chilis in this dish.

⅔ cup of couscous
1 tablespoon bouillon powder
2 teaspoons cumin
1 teaspoon dried Mexican oregano
2 teaspoons dried onion
¼ cup sun-dried tomatoes, finely chopped
½ pasilla chili, seeded and finely shredded
1 garlic clove, minced at home

At Home: Package ingredients in a ziplock bag.

In Camp: Empty contents of bag into serving bowl or cook pot. Stir in *1 cup* of boiling water. Mix well, cover, and let soak for 10 minutes. Fluff with a fork.

Variations: Sprinkling generously with a grated hard cheese will make this a complete meal. Try serving with a Journey Cake (page 60), soup, or a freshly caught baked trout—a true feast.

Chili

Put some cheese in your bowl and pour on some of this chili. It's especially good with Corn Bread (page 112) on a cold ten-thousand-foot night. See Basic Foods (page 7) for lentil types and cooking times.

1 cup lentils
¼ cup tomato powder
2 tablespoons masa
1 tablespoon chili powder
1 tablespoon onion flakes
1 teaspoon cumin
1 teaspoon oregano
½ teaspoon salt
2 garlic cloves, crushed, *or* ¼ teaspoon garlic granules

At Home: Combine ingredients in a ziplock plastic bag.

In Camp: Bring *4 cups* of water to a boil and stir in the lentil mixture. Bring back to a boil. Cover, reduce heat, and simmer for 15 minutes. Use a heat diffuser or stir occasionally to prevent sticking.

Lentil Tomato Stew

A meal with these hearty legumes will replenish your energy. See Basic Foods (page 7) for lentil types and cooking times.

⅔ cup lentils
8 ounces noodles, whole wheat, soy rice, *or* sesame
¼ cup tomato powder
1 tablespoon vegetable bouillon powder *or* 1
    vegetable bouillon cube
2 teaspoons parsley flakes
½ teaspoon salt
¼ teaspoon garlic granules *or* 2 garlic cloves, crushed
dash of pepper

At Home: Combine ingredients in a ziplock plastic bag.

In Camp: Bring *5 cups* of water to a boil and stir in the mixture. Return to a boil. Cover, reduce heat, and simmer for 15 minutes, stirring occasionally.

Lentils & Noodles

The deep flavor of lentils and the comfort of noodles make this a satisfying meal. See Basic Foods (page 7) for lentil types and cooking times.

¾ cup lentils
½ cup noodles of your choice
2 tablespoons whole wheat flour
1 tablespoon onion flakes
½ teaspoon salt
⅛ teaspoon ground cloves
1 bay leaf
dash of pepper
1 tablespoon apple cider vinegar *or* lemon juice

At Home: Combine all ingredients, including vinegar, in a ziplock plastic bag.

In Camp: Bring *4 cups* of water to a boil and stir in the lentil mixture. Return to a boil, reduce heat, and simmer, covered, for 15 minutes. Use a heat diffuser or stir occasionally to prevent sticking.

Asian Rice & Lentils

==============================

Rice and lentils, when eaten together, provide a rich balance of protein. See Basic Foods (page 7) for lentil types and cooking times.

½ cup basmati rice
½ cup lentils
2 tablespoons butter
½ teaspoon salt
½ teaspoon cinnamon
½ teaspoon ginger
½ teaspoon cardamom
2 whole cloves
1 bay leaf
pinch of cayenne (optional)

At Home: Combine ingredients in a ziplock plastic bag.

In Camp: Bring 2½ *cups* of water to a boil and stir in the mixture. Return to a boil, cover, reduce heat, and simmer 20 minutes. Use a heat diffuser if you have one, or stir occasionally to prevent sticking.

Variations: Use Quinoa (page 203) or lentils and Plain Brown Rice (page 180) cooked at home.

Plain Brown Rice

==

makes 2¾ cups

A serving of plain brown rice is a meal unto itself—aromatic, chewy, nutty, and filling. However, brown rice cooked in camp is not very practical, especially at high elevations, where it will take over an hour to cook. But it is possible to have this tasty grain by cooking the rice at home. Try it on the trail with a sauce, as a side dish for fresh fish, or as an accompaniment to a bowl of soup. Kids like it for breakfast with a dollop of butter and maple syrup or honey. Remember that combining brown rice with beans adds protein to a meal.

1 cup brown rice (we prefer short grain)
pinch of salt
2½ cups water

At Home: Bring ingredients to a boil, reduce heat to low, cover, and simmer for about 45 minutes. Don't peek at or stir the rice until it is cooked. Remove from heat. Cool. Package in a ziplock plastic bag.

In Camp: The rice will stay fresh for 2–3 days. If the rice gets sour, rinse it in cold water and drain.

Variations: Add 1–2 tablespoons dried herbs to the water and rice before cooking. Use as a base for soup or stew.

Basmati or Jasmine Rice

The air is perfumed by these lovely rices. Serve with a sauce or as a substitute for any grain.

In Camp: Cook ½ cup rice per person in twice as much water as rice. Add a pinch of salt and a tablespoon of butter or olive oil to the pot. Cover. Simmer for 20–25 minutes. Fluff with a fork.

Variations: Add to the pot 1 tablespoon dried mixed herbs or 2 teaspoons curry powder. Use four times the water and make soup or a stew base.

Instant Wild Rice

serves 2

Instant wild rice is precooked and then dried. It takes 7 minutes to soak in boiled water. Here is a recipe for buttered wild rice with a few variations. (For mail-order information, turn to Food Sources, page 268.)

1 4-ounce package instant wild rice (approximately
    1½ cups)
2–3 tablespoons butter

In Camp: Bring 2 *cups* of water to a boil. Stir in rice, remove from heat, and let soak for approximately 7 minutes. Drain. In a pan, melt butter and stir in soaked rice. Sauté 2–3 minutes.

Variations: Sauté 1–2 crushed garlic cloves in the butter first; add to the rice and water 1 tablespoon mixed dried herbs; serve with a sauce or gravy; use to stuff fresh fish to be steamed; add a handful of nuts and raisins while rice is soaking.

Fruited Wild Rice Salad

serves 2–4

Prepare this salad tasting of wild rice, nuts, and raisins in the morning so it's waiting for you when you return from a day's hiking.

½ cup instant wild rice
2 tablespoons freeze-dried green onions *or* chives
2 tablespoons dried chopped orange peel *or* take an
     orange and grate the peel and then eat the
     orange!
½ cup chopped pecans
½ cup raisins
dash of raspberry vinegar *or* rice vinegar
½ cup vegetable oil
½ cup frozen orange juice concentrate
pepper to taste

At Home: Combine wild rice, dried onions or chives, and dried orange peel in one ziplock bag. In another, combine nuts and raisins. In a small plastic jar, combine vinegar, oil, orange juice concentrate, and pepper for the dressing.

In Camp: Bring 1⅓ cups of salted water to a boil. Add contents of wild rice bag and cook 7 minutes. Add nuts, raisins, and dressing and stir well.

One-Pot Luck

Mushroom Rice

Sauté the shallots, mushrooms, and rice at the beginning, and use the stock to turn this rich, hearty recipe into a whole meal in itself.

¼ cup dried sliced mushrooms
1 medium shallot, diced small
4 cups stock made in camp from bouillon cubes *or* other dried stock mix and including the drained mushroom water
2 cups white rice (aromatic jasmine and basmati are wonderful)
1 teaspoon salt
2 tablespoons olive oil

At Home: Package mushrooms, shallot, and bouillon cubes (or preferred stock base) in separate airtight bags. Package rice and salt in a separate ziplock bag. Carry olive oil separately.

In Camp: Place mushrooms in a cup, cover with water, and let soak for 5–15 minutes. In a pot, sauté shallot in olive oil over low heat until soft. Drain mushrooms (add the water to the stock) and chop. Add to the shallots and briefly sauté together over low heat—they scorch easily. Add rice and stir quickly, allowing rice to get coated with the olive oil and to toast slightly. Add stock, stir, cover, and bring to a boil. Don't peek! When it boils, keep lid on and reduce heat immediately to very low. Use a heat diffuser if you are using a stove with a fierce flame. Cook for 5 minutes, remove from heat, and let stand, covered, for another 5 minutes.

Rice Curry

==========================

Carry along some chapatis to scoop up this sweet and spicy rice.

1 cup basmati rice *or* quinoa
1 tablespoon onion flakes
2 teaspoons curry powder
½ teaspoon salt
handful of dried apricots, raisins, dates, and pears, chopped
handful of whole or chopped almonds, cashews, *or* peanuts

At Home: Combine ingredients in a ziplock plastic bag.

In Camp: Bring *3 cups* of water to a boil and stir in the rice mixture. Return to a boil, cover, reduce heat, and simmer for 20 minutes. Use a heat diffuser to prevent scorching or stir occasionally to prevent sticking. Garnish with coconut or salted peanuts.

Variations: Use bulgur: simmer for 5 minutes, remove from heat, and let stand, covered, 10 minutes. Use millet: toast and crack it at home, simmer for 15 minutes in camp. Use precooked Plain Brown Rice (page 180).

Seaweed Rice

makes 2 cups

This is a basic rice recipe with seaweed added for extra nutrition. However, it varies in flavor depending on your choice of rice and seaweed, and the amount of seaweed you use. Any combination is fragrant, delectable, and nourishing.

1 cup basmati *or* jasmine rice (or baby basmati, which cooks faster)
¼ teaspoon salt (optional)
1 4-by-4-inch piece of kombu or equivalent seaweed *or* ½ cup hijiki or arame
1 teaspoon olive oil

At Home: Combine ingredients in one airtight bag.

In Camp: Pour ingredients in a pot with 2 *cups* of water and bring to a boil. Cover and cook over low heat for 15 minutes. Remove from heat and let stand, covered, for another 5 minutes. If you are using baby basmati rice, reduce cooking time to 10 minutes.

Spinach Cheese Casserole

This hearty dish is filling and high in protein.

1¼ cups basmati rice *or* quinoa
½ cup dehydrated spinach flakes
¼ cup dried mushrooms, minced
2 garlic cloves, minced, *or* ¼ teaspoon garlic granules
½ teaspoon salt
1 6½-ounce can shrimp *or* ½ cup freeze-dried shrimp
½ pound raw-milk cheddar cheese, grated or
      chopped in small chunks, *or* ½ cup grated
      Parmesan cheese

At Home: Combine dry ingredients in a ziplock plastic bag. Carry cheese and shrimp separately.

In Camp: Bring *3 cups* of water to a boil and stir in the rice mixture. Return to a boil, reduce heat, cover, and simmer for 20 minutes. Use a heat diffuser or stir occasionally to prevent sticking. Stir in cheese and shrimp with juice from can. Heat through and serve. If using freeze-dried shrimp, add with the rice mixture.

Variations: Use millet, bulgur, or precooked Plain Brown Rice (page 180).

Macaroni & Cheese

==============================

This classic dish is surprisingly simple to make in camp.

¼ pound cheese (cheddar and/or jack), grated
¼ cup milk powder
1 tablespoon parsley flakes
2 garlic cloves, minced, *or* ¼ teaspoon garlic granules
      or ½ teaspoon garlic powder
8 ounces macaroni (wheat, rice, quinoa, etc.)

At Home: Package the cheese, milk powder, parsley, and garlic in one ziplock plastic bag, and the macaroni in another.

In Camp: Bring 2–3 *cups* of water to a boil and stir in the macaroni. Boil 10 minutes. Drain and stir in the milk and cheese mixture until the cheese is melted.

Variations: Add canned tuna or shrimp; add chopped onion along with macaroni; add a little chili powder and ground cumin; use buckwheat noodles and season with oregano; season with rosemary, basil, or savory; add chopped walnuts.

Alpine Spaghetti

Pesto!

8 ounces angel hair *or* spaghetti
1 tablespoon olive oil *or* butter
1 cup grated Parmesan cheese
3 tablespoons ground dried basil
1 tablespoon parsley flakes
2 garlic cloves, minced, *or* ¼ teaspoon garlic granules

At Home: Package pasta in a ziplock plastic bag. Carry olive oil in a plastic lidded bottle. Combine remaining ingredients in another ziplock plastic bag.

In Camp: Bring *4 cups* of water to a boil and add the pasta. Boil for 3–5 minutes and drain. Add the olive oil and toss. Add the rest of the ingredients and toss again until thoroughly mixed.

Presto Pasta

This is the quickest of all dinners.

8 ounces angel hair pasta
½ teaspoon salt
Asian chili pepper flakes (or other red chili pepper
      flakes) to taste
Parmesan cheese, grated, to taste
¼–⅓ cup olive oil

At Home: Package pasta in one ziplock plastic bag and
the salt, chili flakes, and cheese in another. Carry
olive oil in a bottle with a tight-fitting lid.

In Camp: Bring 4 cups of salted water to a boil. Add
pasta and cook until done, about 3–5 minutes. Drain
and toss with oil, spices, and cheese. Serve hot.

Sun-Dried Tomato Pasta

This is an elegant and satisfying meal for the end of yet another day in paradise.

¼ cup sun-dried tomatoes, chopped
¼ cup pine nuts
½ teaspoon garlic granules
1 tablespoon dried parsley
1 tablespoon dried loose-leaf basil
½ teaspoon salt
pepper to taste
8 ounces angel hair pasta
¼ cup olive oil
1 tablespoon butter (optional)
Parmesan cheese, grated, to taste

At Home: Put tomatoes in a small airtight bag. Put the next six ingredients in another ziplock bag. Pasta may be broken in half or thirds; place in a third bag. Carry oil, butter, and Parmesan cheese separately.

In Camp: Place tomatoes in a small cup and cover with water. Set aside. Boil a pot of salted water for the pasta and cook until done (3–5 minutes). Drain. Pour the water off the tomatoes and combine all remaining ingredients, except the cheese, in the sauté pan, briefly stirring together over the heat. Top with Parmesan cheese.

Spicy Cabbage Noodles

serves 4

Cabbage keeps very well, and this recipe makes it go a long way, satisfying that craving for fresh vegetables.

½ head of cabbage, shredded
1 shallot
1 2-inch piece of ginger
8 ounces bean thread noodles (also called "spring rain") or fine egg noodles
2 tablespoons toasted sesame oil
2 tablespoons olive oil
½ teaspoon Asian chili flakes
3 tablespoons toasted sesame seeds
½ teaspoon salt (optional)
1 tablespoon soy sauce

At Home: Pack the shredded cabbage in an airtight plastic bag. If the ends are dry, the shallot and ginger may be bagged together. If you use bean thread noodles, break them into small pieces. Put noodles in a separate bag. Oils may be bottled together. Package chili flakes, sesame seeds, and salt together. Carry soy sauce separately.

In Camp: Pour enough boiling water over the noodles to just cover them. Cover and wrap pot in a towel or blanket. Let stand for 10 minutes (20 for bean thread noodles); the noodles will cook without further heat. Meanwhile, mince shallot and sauté in the oils for 2 minutes or until soft. Peel and grate ginger, then add to shallots. Add chili flakes, sesame seeds, and salt, and stir quickly. Add the shredded cabbage and continue to stir and cook for another 5–7 minutes. Add soy sauce and stir. Drain noodles and combine with the cabbage mixture. Lift noodles from underneath to coat them with the oils.

Soba Seaweed Salad

The combined aromatic flavors of toasted sesame and seaweed make this a popular backpacker's salad.

½ cup arame seaweed
3–4 tablespoons freeze-dried chives *or* 4 fresh green onions, chopped
16 ounces soba noodles (buckwheat)

Dressing:
½ cup toasted sesame oil
3 tablespoons brown rice vinegar
2 tablespoons maple syrup
1 tablespoon Dijon mustard
2 teaspoons salt

At Home: Combine seaweed and chives in a small plastic bag, or add chives to the dressing. Combine dressing ingredients and stir with a whisk. Carry in a plastic container inside a plastic ziplock bag. Carry noodles separately.

In Camp: Soak seaweed and chives for 7 minutes in enough water to cover them. Meanwhile, cook the soba 5–7 minutes in *4 cups* of salted boiling water and drain. Combine soba, drained seaweed and chives, and dressing and mix well to coat the noodles. May be eaten warm or cool.

Green Noodle Salad

It's a good idea to make this when you have your breakfast fire going; just let it sit in the pot until lunch or dinner. It's filling and is very good for dinner, especially while you wait for soup to cook.

8 ounces artichoke *or* spinach noodles
¼ cup parsley flakes
1 tablespoon onion flakes
½ teaspoon salt
½ teaspoon basil
¼ teaspoon oregano
¼ teaspoon garlic granules

At Home: Combine ingredients in a ziplock plastic bag.

In Camp: Bring 2½ *cups* of water to a boil. Stir in the noodle mixture. Boil for 10 minutes. Toss with Miso Dressing (page 79) or your favorite dressing, and let marinate 1 hour to all day. Or simply coat with 1–2 tablespoons olive oil. Toss again before serving.

Fruit & Noodle Salad

serves 2

This is a surprising and delightful salad to enjoy for lunch or dinner.

8 ounces noodle shells *or* spirals
¾ cup grated Swiss or Jarlsberg cheese *or* ¼ cup
    grated Parmesan cheese
⅓ cup mixed dried fruit, such as chopped apricots,
    raisins, currants
⅓ cup pecans *or* walnuts (toasted if preferred)

Dressing:
¼ cup lemon juice and grated rind of ½ lemon
½ cup olive oil
2 teaspoons Dijon mustard
2 garlic cloves, crushed
salt and pepper to taste

At Home: Package noodles and cheese separately. Combine fruit and nuts in a ziplock plastic bag. Combine dressing ingredients in a plastic bottle; put the bottle in a ziplock plastic bag to prevent leaks.

In Camp: In a large pot, bring *4 cups* of water to a boil. Add noodles and boil for 5–10 minutes. Drain. Add the fruit mixture and the dressing. Cool. Add the cheese. Marinate for 1 hour to all day.

Polenta Cheese Stew

This tasty stew will satisfy your craving for a home-style meal.

½ cup milk powder
½ cup dehydrated corn *or* freeze-dried peas
¼ cup polenta *or* corn grits
1 tablespoon bell pepper flakes
1 bay leaf
1 teaspoon parsley flakes
1 tablespoon onion flakes
1 teaspoon celery flakes
2 garlic cloves, crushed, *or* ¼ teaspoon garlic granules
       or ½ teaspoon garlic powder
1 teaspoon savory
½ teaspoon salt
dash of cayenne
4–6 sun-dried tomatoes
¼ cup sunflower seeds (optional)
¼ pound cheddar cheese, chunked in camp, *or* 1 cup
       grated Parmesan cheese

At Home: Combine all ingredients, except cheese, in a ziplock plastic bag.

In Camp: Bring *4 cups* of water to a boil and stir in the polenta mixture. Return to a boil, cover, reduce heat, and cook for 5–10 minutes. Use a heat diffuser or stir occasionally to prevent sticking. Stir in the cheese and serve.

Polenta Mush

==

Polenta is a special grind of corn that can be found in natural food stores or in any market that sells Italian food. If you can't find polenta, substitute an equal amount of corn grits. Polenta cooks into a thick mush and can be sweet or savory, depending on what you add. When cooled, the mush can be sliced, sautéed, and served with a sauce. The basic recipe is for two servings. Halve, double, triple, etc., the recipe according to your needs.

1 cup polenta *or* corn grits
2 tablespoons soy grits
½ teaspoon salt

At Home: Combine ingredients in a ziplock plastic bag.

In Camp: Bring *4 cups* of water to a boil. Stir in the polenta mixture, return to a boil, cover, and reduce heat to low. Use a heat diffuser if necessary to prevent scorching. Cook 5–10 minutes without stirring.

Cereal: Prepare the basic recipe. Then stir in and heat through any of the following to taste: dried fruit, nuts, seeds, milk powder, cinnamon, honey, butter, maple syrup.

One-Pot Meal: Prepare the basic recipe. Then stir in any one of the following combinations and heat through. If using cheese or seafood, stir it in just before serving.

- ½ cup walnuts *or* pecans, ¼ pound cheddar cheese, cubed, and fresh garlic and onions to taste

- chili powder, cumin, oregano, onions, garlic to taste, and jack cheese

- a 6½-ounce can of albacore tuna and dill to taste

Polenta Mush Cakes: Prepare the basic recipe and allow it to cool. Slice or form into patties, and sauté in a little butter or oil. Serve with maple syrup or honey.

Doug's Bulgur

serves 2

Bulgur is precooked cracked wheat, which makes it a quick-cooking dinner base especially good for building seafood variations.

1 cup bulgur
2 tablespoons soy grits
1 tablespoon vegetable bouillon powder *or* 1
    vegetable bouillon cube
2 garlic cloves, crushed, *or* ¼ teaspoon garlic granules
    or ½ teaspoon garlic powder
1–2 bay leaves

At Home: Combine ingredients in a ziplock plastic bag.

In Camp: Bring 2–4 *cups* of water (depending on whether you're making a stew or soup) to a boil. Stir in the bulgur mixture and return to a boil. Remove from heat, cover, and let stand for 15 minutes. Gently reheat if necessary.

Variations: Add small handfuls of your favorite dried vegetables; add a chopped fresh onion and/or carrot; add your favorite mixed herbs or soy sauce. Just before serving, stir in canned albacore tuna, salmon, mackerel, shrimp, or crab.

Spanish Bulgur

This takes only minutes to cook and is a great grain dish. Serve it with Fish Patties (page 218), or melt in some cheese.

1 cup bulgur
¼ cup dried mushrooms, chopped
1 tablespoon tomato powder
1 tablespoon celery flakes
1 tablespoon onion flakes
1 tablespoon dried bell pepper
2 garlic cloves, minced, *or* ¼ teaspoon garlic granules
      or ½ teaspoon garlic powder
1 teaspoon cumin
½ teaspoon powdered red chilies
pinch of salt

At Home: Combine all ingredients in a ziplock plastic bag.

In Camp: Bring 2½ *cups* of water to a boil. Stir in the bulgur mixture, cover, reduce heat, and simmer for 2–5 minutes. Remove from heat and let stand for 5–10 minutes.

Mushroom Bulgur

serves 2

Hearty mushrooms and grains are a perfect dinner combination.

1 cup bulgur
¼ cup dried mushrooms, chopped
3 tablespoons toasted sesame seeds
1 tablespoon onion flakes
1 vegetable bouillon cube *or* 1 tablespoon vegetable
    bouillon powder
1 tablespoon celery flakes
1 tablespoon parsley flakes
1 teaspoon dried savory

At Home: Combine ingredients in a ziplock plastic bag.

In Camp: Place ingredients in a cook pot and add 2–2½ *cups* of water. Bring to a boil, cover, reduce heat, and simmer for 5 minutes. Remove from heat. Set aside, covered, for 10 minutes to complete the cooking.

Bulgur with Sage

This is an earthy grain dish. Serve with Mushroom Sauce (page 163).

1 cup bulgur
2 tablespoons celery flakes
1 tablespoon onion flakes
2 garlic cloves, crushed, *or* ¼ teaspoon garlic granules
     or ½ teaspoon garlic powder
½ teaspoon each sage and thyme
salt to taste
2 tablespoons peanut butter or any roasted nut butter

At Home: Combine dry ingredients in a ziplock plastic bag. Package the peanut butter in a squeeze tube or a wide-mouth plastic bottle with a lid.

In Camp: Bring *2 cups* of water to a boil. Stir in the bulgur mixture. Return to a boil, reduce heat, cover, and simmer for 5 minutes. Remove from heat, stir in the peanut butter, and let stand, covered, for 10 minutes.

One-Pot Grain & Seafood

serves 2

There are many possibilities for this one-pot meal: using different grains and/or noodles and adding your choice of seasonings and seafood.

1 cup bulgur *or* precooked brown rice
1 tablespoon tomato powder
1 tablespoon celery flakes
1 tablespoon dried bell pepper
1 tablespoon onion flakes
2 garlic cloves, crushed, *or* ¼ tablespoon garlic
    granules *or* ½ tablespoon garlic powder
1 tablespoon curry powder *or* chili powder *or* mixed
    herbs *or* garam masala
4–6 sun-dried tomatoes, chopped
1 6½-ounce can seafood of your choice
cheese of your choice, grated

At Home: Combine dry ingredients in a ziplock plastic bag. (If using precooked brown rice, follow the instructions on page 180 and package separately.) Carry the seafood and cheese separately.

In Camp: Bring 2½ cups of water to a boil and stir in the bulgur mixture. Return to a boil, reduce heat, and simmer for 5 minutes. Remove from heat, stir in seafood and cheese, and let stand 10 minutes. Stir before serving.

Variations: You may also use millet or basmati rice. If you're using millet, toast and crack it at home and increase the cooking time in camp to 15–20 minutes. If you're using basmati rice, increase the cooking time to 20 minutes.

Tabouli

Make this in the morning and let it cool in the shade until lunch or dinner. Toss and serve with Falafel (page 67), pocket bread, or Tahini Dipping Sauce (page 81).

1 cup bulgur
1 tablespoon onion flakes
¼ cup parsley flakes
1 tablespoon dried mint
black pepper and salt to taste
4–6 sun-dried tomatoes
½ cup olive oil
½ cup lemon juice

At Home: Combine dry ingredients in a ziplock plastic bag. Carry oil and lemon juice together in a plastic bottle. Put the bottle in a ziplock plastic bag to prevent leaks.

In Camp: Bring *2 cups* of water to a boil. Stir in the bulgur mixture, cover, and remove from heat. Let stand for 10 minutes. Add the oil and lemon juice and toss. Let stand until cool. Toss again before serving.

Quinoa

Pronounced *keenwa,* this is a grain that comes from the Andean regions of South America. Quinoa was a staple food of the Inca civilization and is still known as the "mother grain." It contains more protein than any other grain, is a complete protein by itself, and is also high in fiber, minerals, and vitamins. Its high nutritional value and its quick and easy preparation make it a perfect food for backpacking and camping. It can replace any grain in any recipe; just remember to shorten the cooking time to 15 minutes.

1 cup quinoa
2 cups water

In Camp: Rinse quinoa in cold water and drain. Place in a cook pot with *2 cups* of water and bring to a boil. Reduce heat, cover, and cook for 10–15 minutes, or until all the water is absorbed. Use a heat diffuser or stir occasionally to prevent sticking. The grains will turn from white to transparent.

Wakame Quinoa

No, it is not a new dance! Fluffy and delicate in flavor, this would be a good accompaniment to freshly fried fish or would work well combined with a can of tiny shrimp.

1 cup quinoa
½ teaspoon salt (optional)
½ onion, diced small in camp, *or* 1½ teaspoons onion
    flakes
½ cup toasted wakame, broken into small pieces
1 tablespoon olive oil
soy sauce to taste

At Home: Combine quinoa and salt in an airtight bag. Package half onion and wakame in another bag. Bottle olive oil and soy sauce separately.

In Camp: Sauté onion and wakame in olive oil for 2 minutes, or until onions are just starting to brown. Add *2 tablespoons* of water and sauté another 2 minutes, or until onion is soft but still has a little crunch. Combine quinoa, *2 cups* of water, and wakame mixture and bring to a boil. Cover, reduce heat, and simmer 5 minutes. Remove from heat and let sit, covered, for 15 minutes. Stir and serve.

Mountain Gruel

This is a basic recipe with many options: you can make it into a soup, cereal, one-pot meal, or pudding.

½ cup rolled oats
½ cup rolled wheat
2 tablespoons soy grits
½ teaspoon salt

At Home: Combine ingredients in a ziplock plastic bag.

In Camp: Combine oat mixture with *2 cups* of water and bring to a boil over moderate heat, stirring occasionally. Reduce heat and cook slowly for 5–10 minutes.

Cereal: Just before serving, stir in any combination of the following to taste: raisins or other dried fruit, nuts or seeds, raw wheat germ, milk powder, cinnamon, honey, maple syrup.

Toasted Cereal: Before adding water to the basic recipe, toast grains first by stirring constantly in a dry pan over moderate heat. The grains will have a toasted aroma. Then proceed as in the basic recipe. Garnish with Sesame Salt (page 84), soy sauce, nuts, or seeds.

Soup: Prepare the basic recipe but add *4 cups* of water instead of 2. Along with the water add any one of the following combinations to taste: tomato powder, miso, cumin, and oregano; vegetable bouillon cube, onion, and garlic; Parmesan cheese, milk powder, garlic, and basil.

Dessert: Prepare the basic recipe and add any combination of the following to taste: vanilla, milk powder, allspice, cloves, nutmeg, and/or ginger, molasses, honey, or maple syrup, Home-Dried Apples (page 29).

Millet Pilaf

━━━━━━━━━━━━━━━━━━━━━━━━━━━

serves 2

Pour Curry Sauce (page 164) or Nut Butter Sauce (page 165) over this for a great meal.

1 cup millet
3 tablespoons butter
2 tablespoons raisins
1 2-inch cinnamon stick
5 whole cloves
1 fresh onion, chopped in camp
1 fresh carrot, chopped in camp

At Home: In a frying pan over moderate heat, toast millet to a golden brown, stirring frequently. Cool, then crack in a blender. Combine the cracked millet with butter, raisins, cinnamon, and cloves in a ziplock plastic bag. Carry the carrot and onion separately.

In Camp: Bring 2½ *cups* of water to a boil. Stir in the millet mixture and chopped vegetables. Return to a boil, reduce heat, cover, and simmer for 15–20 minutes. Use a heat diffuser or stir occasionally to prevent sticking.

Swiss Fondue

This is a romantic meal for an overnight trip or a cross-country ski lunch.

2 cups (10 ounces) grated Emmentaler cheese
2 cups (10 ounces) grated Gruyère cheese
3 tablespoons kirsch
1 tablespoon cornstarch
1½ cups dry white wine
1 garlic clove
1 teaspoon lemon juice
white pepper and grated nutmeg to taste
French bread for serving

At Home: Package cheeses in a ziplock plastic bag. Combine kirsch and cornstarch in a separate ziplock plastic bag. Carry garlic, lemon juice, and seasoning separately. Carry a lemon and a bottle of wine. Don't forget the corkscrew!

In Camp: Cut the garlic in half and rub the inside of a cook pot with the cut surface. Use a thick-bottomed pot, or if you're using a thin pot, keep the flame very low or use a heat diffuser. Heat the wine and lemon juice carefully. Add the cheese gradually, stirring continuously in a figure-eight motion. When the mixture is bubbling, add the kirsch and cornstarch. Cook 2–3 minutes. Season to taste with pepper and nutmeg.

To keep the fondue warm but not overcooked, place the fondue pot in another pan with a few inches of water. Place the pans over the stove and keep the water at a simmer.

To eat, dip chunks of bread, skewered on a fork or chopstick.

Beer Fondue

==

Can't get to the pub tonight? Try this rich fondue and do some stargazing.

2 cups (8 ounces) grated cheddar cheese
2 tablespoons cornstarch
½ teaspoon dry mustard
1 cup beer, preferably ale
1–2 cloves garlic, crushed in camp
French bread

At Home: Package cheese in a ziplock plastic bag. Combine the cornstarch and mustard in a separate bag. Carry beer and garlic separately.

In Camp: Place beer, cheese, and garlic in a thick-bottomed pan, or use a heat diffuser. Cook over low heat, stirring constantly, until the cheese has melted. Blend cornstarch and mustard with a little extra beer or water. Add to the fondue and stir until thickened. (See Swiss Fondue, page 207, for more on heating cheese mixture.)

To eat, dip chunks of bread, skewered on a fork or chopstick.

Burritos

There are so many things to put in a flour tortilla—from beans and rice to vegetables to cheese to sweet things (see Sweet-Treat Burritos for Kids, page 237). Try flavored tortillas—spinach, sun-dried tomato, garlic and herb, and more!

Basic burrito: Heat the filling and set aside. Fry the tortilla in a little olive oil. Place the filling of your choice in the center of the tortilla, start rolling, fold the sides toward the center, and finish rolling.

Filling ideas:

- Stuffed Portobello (page 89)

- leftover One-Pot meals and cheese

- broken-up Walnut Cheese Burgers (page 65) with wasabi

- Falafel (page 67) with Tahini Dipping Sauce (page 81)

- lentils and rice with grated cheese, sprouts, and soaked sun-dried tomatoes

- All Dal-ed Up Dip (page 170), and grated cheddar cheese

- basmati rice and Cilantro Lime Dressing (page 79)

- Mushroom Rice (page 183), and grated aged Gruyère cheese

Fish & Seafood

Fresh, canned, or dried—a little fish or seafood expands the dynamics of food for the pack. Fresh trout, stocked by fishery departments, can be caught (if you are lucky!) in mountain streams. (Be certain to follow Fish and Game rules and regulations.) Many fish and seafood products are now available canned in most grocery stores—tuna, salmon, shrimp, smoked oysters, crab, and much more. Asian food stores offer interesting and tasty dried fish and seafood—iriko (dried fish), bonito flakes, and calamari are just a start. Explore, have fun, and enjoy!

Thai Crab Cakes

This taste of Thailand works well with Mushroom Ginger Noodle Soup (page 124).

1 cup coarsely crushed saltine crackers
2 teaspoons dried cilantro
2 teaspoons dried basil
1 teaspoon curry powder
½ teaspoon Asian chili flakes
1 tablespoon olive oil
1 tablespoon butter
⅓ cup coconut milk
1 teaspoon fish sauce (Thai Kitchen or other)
1 6½-ounce can crabmeat

At Home: Combine crackers and spices in an airtight bag. Carry oil and butter together in a small container. Combine coconut milk and fish sauce and carry in one plastic bottle. Carry crabmeat separately.

In Camp: Toss together lightly all ingredients except oil and butter (include the liquid from the crab), and shape into four patties about ½ inch thick. Sauté in the oil and butter until browned, about 3 minutes on each side.

Clams over Pasta

==

serves 2

This is a favorite—so simple and gratifying.

8 ounces angel hair *or* other quick-cooking pasta
6–8 garlic cloves, minced at home
1 tablespoon parsley flakes
⅛ teaspoon Asian chili flakes (optional)
2 tablespoons butter (or 4 tablespoons olive oil total)
2–4 tablespoons olive oil
1 tablespoon flour
salt and pepper to taste
1 6½-ounce can chopped clams
juice from the can of clams and enough water to
        make 1 cup liquid

At Home: Package pasta in an airtight bag. Combine garlic, parsley, and chili flakes in a separate airtight bag. Combine butter and oil in a small plastic container. Twist the flour, salt, and pepper up in a piece of waxed paper or plastic wrap and carry separately. Carry the clams separately.

In Camp: Bring *4 cups* of water to a boil. Add the pasta and cook 3–5 minutes. Drain and leave, covered, in the pot. Sauté the garlic, parsley, and chili flakes in the butter and oil. Cook until they are soft, but not brown, about 3 minutes. Add flour, salt, and pepper and sauté 2–3 minutes, stirring constantly. Slowly stir in the water and liquid from the clams. Add clams last, stir, and serve hot over pasta.

Fish & Seafood

Salmon in Tomato Orange Sauce

serves 4

Surprise your friends in the backcountry with this delightful meal. Serve over pasta, rice, or steamed Corn Bread (page 112). Serves two as a chowder with Singing Hinnies (page 115).

¼ cup tomato powder
3 tablespoons flour
1 tablespoon onion flakes
⅓ cup dried mushrooms, chopped fine
2 garlic cloves, crushed, *or* ¼ teaspoon garlic granules
    or ½ teaspoon garlic powder
1 teaspoon fresh *or* dried grated orange rind
½ teaspoon salt
4–6 sun-dried tomatoes, chopped
pinch of cayenne
1 6½-ounce can salmon

At Home: Combine dry ingredients in a ziplock plastic bag. Carry salmon separately.

In Camp: Place all ingredients in a cook pot and stir in 2½ cups of water. Bring to a boil over moderate heat, stirring constantly. Reduce heat, cover, and simmer for 2–3 minutes.

Variations: Replace the salmon with any desired seafood.

Shrimp Curry

Serve with a hot bread or over basmati rice.

¼ cup tomato powder
5 teaspoons curry powder
1 tablespoon parsley flakes
½ teaspoon cumin seeds, crushed
½ teaspoon coriander seeds, crushed
½ teaspoon ginger
½ teaspoon tarragon (optional)
1 tablespoon onion flakes
2 garlic cloves, minced, *or* ¼ teaspoon garlic granules
 or ½ teaspoon garlic powder
1 tablespoon olive oil
2 teaspoons tamari
1 6½-ounce can shrimp

At Home: Combine dry ingredients in a ziplock plastic bag. Carry oil, tamari, and shrimp separately.

In Camp: Sauté dry ingredients in olive oil for 1 minute. Quickly stir in 2 *cups* of water and bring to a boil. Reduce heat, cover, and simmer for 5–10 minutes. Add shrimp and tamari, and heat through.

Variations: Replace shrimp with any seafood of your choice.

Anchovy Spaghetti

serves 2

A backpacker visiting from Switzerland shared this recipe. You have to *love* anchovies.

8 ounces spaghetti
1 2-ounce can of anchovies in oil
2 large garlic cloves, crushed in camp

At Home: Carry ingredients in a plastic ziplock bag.

In Camp: Bring *4 cups* of water to a boil and add spaghetti. Boil until tender, about 10 minutes. Drain, and consider making a quick bowl of soup from this liquid by adding a bouillon cube. Pour the anchovy oil into a pan and cook the crushed garlic until it sizzles. Drop in the anchovies, warming them as you break them into smallish pieces. Add the drained spaghetti and toss to combine.

Variation: Substitute angel hair pasta for shorter cooking time (3–5 minutes).

Shrimp Anchovy Pasta

serves 4

This quick, easy dinner has a wonderful mild seafood flavor.

16 ounces angel hair pasta
1 tablespoon dried parsley flakes
2 large garlic cloves
2 tablespoons olive oil
1½-ounce tube anchovy paste
1 4-ounce can tiny shrimp
green onions, finely sliced (optional)

At Home: Pack pasta in an airtight plastic bag. Parsley flakes may be wrapped in a small piece of plastic wrap. Carry other items separately.

In Camp: Cook pasta in *4 cups* boiling salted water (3–5 minutes). Drain and set aside. Mince the garlic and sauté in olive oil briefly until soft. Add full tube of anchovy paste and stir quickly. Add shrimp and stir again. Add pasta to the pot and toss well to coat. Top with green onions.

Crab à la King

Here you have the luxury of crab in a complete meal!

½ cup grated Parmesan cheese
½ cup milk powder
4 tablespoons flour
2 tablespoons dried chives
1½ tablespoons dried bell pepper
2 garlic cloves, minced
¼ teaspoon nutmeg
pinch of cayenne
6–8 sun-dried tomatoes, chopped
1 6½-ounce can crabmeat
8 ounces spinach egg noodles

At Home: Combine ingredients, except the crab and noodles, in a ziplock plastic bag. Carry the noodles and crab separately.

In Camp: Cook the noodles in *4 cups* of boiling water for 7–10 minutes, drain, and set aside. Empty contents of ziplock bag into the cook pot and gradually stir in *2 cups* of water. Bring to a boil over moderate heat, stirring constantly. Reduce heat, cover, and simmer 3–5 minutes. Stir in crabmeat, with juice from the can, and noodles, heat through, and serve.

Fish Patties

Dip these light fish cakes in Miso Mustard Sauce (page 158).

¼ cup raw wheat germ, plus extra for coating
¼ cup milk powder
1 teaspoon dill weed
1 tablespoon olive oil, if using leftover fish
1 6½-ounce can albacore tuna or other canned fish
    (packed in oil) *or* 1½ cups leftover cooked fish

At Home: Combine dry ingredients in a ziplock plastic bag. Carry fish and oil separately.

In Camp: Drain oil from canned fish into a pan. In a bowl, mix fish with ¼ cup wheat germ, the milk powder, dill weed, and *1 tablespoon* of water. Form into patties ½ inch thick and 1½ inches in diameter, then coat with extra wheat germ. Heat oil till hot and fry patties slowly on both sides, about 10–15 minutes total. Serve with Sweet and Sour Sauce (page 154), Curry Sauce (page 164), or Miso Mustard Sauce (page 158).

Variations: Add leftover cooked grain to these patties and they will serve four. Simply double the dill, add ¼ teaspoon salt, 1 tablespoon curry powder, and another tablespoon of water (depending on the moistness of the grain). Cook as above (you may need to use more oil), and serve with soy sauce or mustard.

Baked Trout

This is a good recipe for one of the first nights out, when you still might have a baked potato left and the fishing has been fine.

4 medium-size trout, or enough fish for two people
½ teaspoon thyme
salt and pepper to taste
1 baked potato, cubed in camp
butter to taste

Lay out two generous pieces of foil. Place clean fish, enough for one serving, on each piece of foil. Season with thyme, salt, and pepper. Scatter the potato cubes around the fish and dot with butter. Seal the foil with the seams on top. Pour about ½ *inch* of water into a pan. Bring to a simmer. Put in the foil packages, cover, and cook at a simmer for 20–30 minutes. The time required depends on the thickness of the fish. Eat right from the package.

Baked Trout with Grain Stuffing

----

serves 2

Dress this trout dish up with delectable Marinara Sauce (page 152).

½ cup instant wild rice *or* bulgur
1 tablespoon parsley flakes
1 teaspoon dill
salt to taste
4 tablespoons butter *or* olive oil
1 lemon, sliced
½ onion, sliced thin
enough clean trout for two

At Home: Combine the rice or bulgur, seasonings, and half the butter or oil in a ziplock plastic bag. Package lemon, onion slices, and remaining 2 tablespoons butter or oil together in a separate ziplock bag.

In Camp: Bring *1 cup* of water to a boil. Stir in rice or bulgur mixture, cover, and set aside to soak for 15 minutes. Lay out two generous pieces of foil. Place clean fish, enough for one serving, on each piece of foil. Stuff the cavity of each fish with grain mixture. Scatter any extra grain around the fish. Dot the fish with remaining butter and top with the slices of onion and lemon. Seal the foil with the seams on top. In a frying pan, bring *½ inch* of water to a simmer. Put in the foil packages, cover, and cook at a simmer for 20–30 minutes, or until the fish is tender. The time required depends on the thickness of the fish. Eat right from the package.

Basic Fried Trout

We always carry a bag of breading mixture for frying trout. Here are a few combinations that we enjoy:

cornmeal; salt, pepper, sage to taste
1 part cornmeal, 1 part corn flour; salt, pepper to
     taste
whole wheat flour; salt, pepper to taste
whole wheat flour; salt, pepper, garlic granules,
     sesame seeds to taste

Clean freshly caught fish and, while still wet, roll it in breading and fry. Fish will be done when the flesh is no longer translucent and flakes away when pried with a fork. (The time required depends on the thickness of the fish.) Sprinkle on a little lemon juice, if you like.

Ben's Fried Trout

Wash and clean fresh-caught trout, leaving it a little moist. Sprinkle a combination of garlic granules, salt, and pepper on one side, and put that side down in a hot frying pan with a little oil. While trout cooks, sprinkle more of the same on the other side. Turn, and fry until done.

Iriko

If you get a chance to go to Chinatown, or to a store that carries Chinese or Japanese products, you might see these small dried fish, about 2 inches long. They are very lightweight and a real treat for a snack. They also are very high in protein, as you eat the fish whole, bones and all.

Oil the bottom of a frying pan, and put in a handful of the dried fish. Brown until toasty and crunchy, sprinkle with soy sauce, and stir. Remove from pan and cool on a plate.

Desserts

Remember celebrations and children! Make a surprise birthday cake, snow ice cream, or that little something sweet after dinner.

High Mountain Pie

This is a favorite of ours. It can be baked as a cake or served like shortcake.

Group 1:
2 cups mixed dried fruit: apricots, apples, figs,
        prunes, raisins, pears, pineapple, dates
large handful of walnuts *or* pecans
1 tablespoon honey
1 teaspoon cinnamon

Group 2:
1 cup brown rice flour
¼ cup raw wheat germ
2 tablespoons milk powder
1 teaspoon baking powder
½ teaspoon cinnamon
½ teaspoon salt
¼ teaspoon nutmeg
2 tablespoons honey
2 tablespoons butter

At Home: Combine Group 1 ingredients in a ziplock plastic bag. Combine Group 2 ingredients, rub in the butter with your fingertips, and package in another ziplock bag.

In Camp: Place Group 1 ingredients in a frying pan with enough water to cover the fruit. Cook over low heat, covered, for 10 minutes. Stir occasionally and add more water as necessary.

Add ½ *cup* of water to the Group 2 ingredients and stir to combine. Remove fruit mixture from heat, and pour batter over it. Cover pan tightly with aluminum foil, crimping it over the pan edges. Place the pan over low heat. (It is a good idea to use a heat diffuser.) Bake for 30 minutes. The crust should be springy to the touch. Serve warm.

Variations: Cook the fruit as above. Make pancake batter by adding more water until batter reaches desired consistency. Cook it in a frying pan as pancakes. Pour the fruit over the pancakes and serve hot.

Applesauce

serves 2

Make a lot of this apple dish and slather it on pancakes, Boston Brown Bread (page 55), or crackers with peanut butter.

2 cups Home-Dried Apples (page 29), chopped
1 tablespoon honey

In Camp: Place apples in a cook pot and add enough water to just barely cover them. Simmer until apples are soft and saucy. Add honey. Serve warm or cold.

Variations: Add ½ teaspoon cinnamon, a squeeze of lemon, ¼ cup raisins, or nuts. Let simmer with apples.

Skillet Brownies

==

Treat your camp-mates to these rich, chocolaty, and easy-to-make brownies. Mix all the ingredients at home and just add water in camp.

1⅓ cups unbleached white flour *or* whole wheat
    pastry flour
¾ cup cocoa
½ cup dark brown sugar
¼ cup white sugar
1 teaspoon baking powder
¼ teaspoon salt
2 tablespoons butter
2 tablespoons canola oil
1 teaspoon vanilla
½ cup chocolate chips
¼ cup walnuts *or* pecans, chopped

At Home: Combine first six ingredients and mix well. Cut in butter and oil to a cornmeal-like consistency, making sure to coat all the dry ingredients. Add vanilla and mix well. Stir in chocolate chips and nuts. Carry in an airtight bag.

In Camp: Pour contents of bag into a bowl. Add ½ *cup* of water and mix well, gently kneading in water with the back of a spoon. Dough will form into a ball and begin to pull away from sides of bowl. Lightly oil a skillet and place over low heat (use a heat diffuser to keep brownies from scorching). Drop dough from a spoon or form into 1-inch balls and gently flatten into disks. Cover skillet and bake 5 minutes on each side. You may need to turn brownies often to prevent scorching.

Apple Crisp

This is delicious and surprisingly easy to make. Everybody loves it.

¼ pound Home-Dried Apples (page 29)
½ teaspoon cinnamon
big pinch of nutmeg
squeeze of lemon
1 cup rolled oats
¼ cup whole wheat flour
2 tablespoons butter
2 teaspoons honey
¼ teaspoon salt

At Home: Combine apples, cinnamon, and nutmeg, and squeeze in lemon juice. Package in a ziplock plastic bag. Combine the remaining ingredients in another ziplock plastic bag, mixing well.

In Camp: Soak apple mixture in *1½–2 cups* water for 10 minutes. Turn the mixture into a cook pot, sprinkle on oat mixture, and cover. Place over low heat. Use a heat diffuser to prevent scorching, and cook for 15–20 minutes.

Apple Barley Pudding

Try this wonderful dessert after a light dinner.

1 cup rolled barley *or* oats
1 cup Home-Dried Apples (page 29), chopped
½ cup raisins
handful of whole walnuts, almonds, pecans, and/or
    hazelnuts
1 teaspoon cinnamon
½ teaspoon nutmeg
dash of cloves (optional)
honey to taste

At Home: Combine ingredients in a ziplock plastic bag.

In Camp: Place ingredients in a cook pot and add 3 *cups* of water. Bring to a boil over moderate heat, cover, and reduce heat to low. Simmer 5–10 minutes. Serve hot.

Tapioca Fruit Pudding

This is a bit like Stewed Fruit Sauce (page 167), but with a texture and flavor all its own.

2 cups dried fruit and chopped nuts of your choice
3 tablespoons tapioca
1 tablespoon rose hip powder
1 tablespoon honey
juice of 1 lemon *or* lime

At Home: Combine ingredients in a ziplock plastic bag.

In Camp: Place fruit mixture in a cook pot and stir in 2½ *cups* of water. Let stand for 5 minutes to 1 hour. Bring to a boil, stirring constantly. Cook 5–10 minutes. Let stand to cool, or serve warm.

Creamy Tapioca Pudding

serves 2

Don't forget this classic dessert, which is great on the trail!

⅔ cup milk powder
3 tablespoons tapioca
1 tablespoon honey
1 teaspoon vanilla
pinch of salt

At Home: Combine ingredients in a ziplock plastic bag.

In Camp: Place tapioca mixture in a cook pot. Slowly stir in *2 cups* of water, and let stand for 5 minutes. Bring to a boil, stirring constantly. Remove from heat. Serve warm, or let stand to cool.

Variation: Add 2 tablespoons carob or cocoa powder to the dry ingredients.

Cup of Custard

serves 2-4

This dessert brings back memories of childhood. Add fruit, nuts, or coconut for four servings, or pour it over Golden Delights (page 232).

½ cup milk powder
1 tablespoon cornstarch
1-2 tablespoons date sugar *or* honey
1 teaspoon vanilla (optional)

At Home: Combine ingredients in a ziplock plastic bag. If you are using vanilla, stir it into the honey or date sugar before adding these ingredients to the bag.

In Camp: Put ingredients in a cook pot. Slowly add *1 cup* of water, stirring constantly. Bring to a simmer over low heat, still stirring. Simmer for 2-3 minutes to cook the cornstarch. Serve warm or cold.

Variation: For a chocolate custard, add 2 tablespoons of cocoa to the ingredients mixture at home.

Golden Delights

====================================

serves 4

This orangey steamed pudding is a filling dessert after a light meal. Serve it with Cup of Custard (page 231).

1 cup unbleached white flour
2 teaspoons baking powder
1½ teaspoons dried orange peel
handful of golden raisins
3 tablespoons oil *or* butter
⅓ cup honey
1 egg
1 orange *or* 8 apricot halves
2 tablespoons syrup *or* honey *or* jam

At Home: Combine dry ingredients and raisins in a ziplock plastic bag. Pour the oil and honey into a plastic bottle. To avoid spills, put the bottle in another ziplock plastic bag. Carry the egg and orange or apricot halves separately.

In Camp: In a bowl, add *3 tablespoons* of water to the oil or butter and honey. Add dry ingredients and egg and mix well. If you brought an orange, slice it thinly. Place orange slices, with the skin on, or apricot halves on the bottom of an oiled medium-size pot. Pour on the syrup, honey, or jam. Pour the pudding batter on top of that and cover with a tight-fitting lid or foil (tied on). Steam for 30–40 minutes, following the basic steaming directions on page 18. The pudding should be springy to the touch. Make sure the lid is tied on tightly, or steam will get into the pudding and make it soggy.

Pineapple Upside-Down Cake

serves 2–4

This cake is great for a backcountry birthday. Don't forget the candles!

½ cup pastry flour
⅓ cup brown rice flour
¼ cup milk powder
¼ cup raw wheat germ
1 teaspoon baking powder
¼ cup honey
2 tablespoons oil
1 teaspoon vanilla
4–6 dried pineapple rings

Topping:
2 tablespoons butter
¼ cup honey
½ cup walnuts *or* pecans

At Home: Combine first five ingredients in a ziplock plastic bag. Combine honey, oil, and vanilla in a plastic bottle. Put the bottle in another ziplock plastic bag to prevent spills. Carry pineapple separately. In a lidded container, combine butter, honey, and nuts for the topping.

In Camp: Add oil mixture to the dry ingredients with ⅓ *cup* of water. Mix well. Place pineapple rings, whole or broken into small pieces, in an oiled 7–8-inch pan. Pour topping mixture over the pineapple, then pour batter over that. Cover tightly, and bake at low heat, using a heat diffuser if necessary, for 20–25 minutes, or until cake is springy to the touch.

Steamed Chocolate Fudge Pudding

================================

serves 2

This pudding is pure chocolate decadence!

½ cup flour
1 teaspoon baking powder
2 tablespoons cocoa
2 tablespoons chopped walnuts (optional)
⅓ cup butter
¼ cup honey
1 teaspoon vanilla
1 egg

Topping:
½ cup honey
2 tablespoons cocoa

At Home: Combine flour, baking powder, cocoa, and nuts in a ziplock bag. Combine the butter, honey, and vanilla in a plastic bottle. Carry the egg separately. Make sure you have the correct size pot, at least 5 inches in diameter with a tightly fitting lid, or carry foil to cover it. Combine the topping ingredients in another plastic bottle. To avoid possible spills, carry the bottles together in a ziplock bag.

In Camp: Combine flour mixture, butter mixture, egg, and 1 *tablespoon* of water. Mix well. Place the batter in a medium-size oiled pot. Combine ¾ *cup* of hot water with topping mixture. Pour on top of batter. Place the lid on or make a lid of foil. Steam for 30–40 minutes, following the basic steaming instructions on page 18. Enjoy the pudding while it's warm.

Alternative cooking method: Follow the directions for "In Camp," but put the batter in an oiled metal cake-ring pan. Pour on topping mixture and cover tightly with foil. Bake over low heat, using a heat diffuser between stove and pan, for about 20 minutes. Serve warm from the pan.

Gingerbread

----

serves 2

This is a delicious, moist, steamed bread. It does take 60 minutes to steam, but it is well worth the wait. If you just can't wait or your fuel is low, steam for 30 minutes for a "ginger goo pudding." Serve the leftover gingerbread cold the next day with sharp cheddar cheese. An epicurean delight!

1½ cups whole wheat flour *or* unbleached white flour
2 tablespoons buttermilk powder
1 tablespoon ginger
1 teaspoon cinnamon
1 teaspoon baking soda
½ cup unsulfured molasses
¼ cup honey (optional)
¼ cup butter
1 egg (optional)

At Home: Combine dry ingredients in a ziplock plastic bag. Combine molasses, honey, and butter in a plastic bottle. Carry the bottle in another ziplock plastic bag to prevent spills. Carry the egg separately.

In Camp: Combine the two mixtures (and egg, if using) and mix in ⅓–½ *cup* of water. Stir well. Pour into a lightly greased medium-size cook pot. Follow steaming directions on page 18. The gingerbread will take a full hour to steam. It should be springy to the touch. If it's not, cover again and steam for 10 minutes more.

Spice Cake

Honey and spice and everything nice!

¾ cup pastry flour
¼ cup brown rice flour
¼ cup raw wheat germ
¼ cup milk powder
1 teaspoon baking powder
1 teaspoon cinnamon
½ teaspoon allspice
¼ teaspoon nutmeg
pinch of cloves
pinch of salt
small handful each of chopped walnuts, raisins,
        chopped dried apples
⅓ cup honey
¼ cup oil
1 teaspoon vanilla

At Home: Combine dry ingredients and fruit in a ziplock plastic bag. Combine honey, oil, and vanilla in a plastic bottle. To avoid spills, put the bottle in another ziplock plastic bag.

In Camp: Combine the two mixtures, and add ⅓ *cup* of water. Mix well. Pour batter into oiled skillet or metal ring mold. Cover tightly with lid or foil, and bake over low heat, using a heat diffuser, for 20–30 minutes. Cake is done when springy to the touch.

Date Walnut Topping

makes approximately ¾ cup

Serve this as a sweet topping on Meal Cakes (page 143), bread, or pancakes—hot or cold.

½ cup dates, pitted and sliced
¼ cup walnuts, chopped fine

In Camp: Place ingredients in a cook pot with *½ cup* of water. Stir over low heat until warmed through.

Sweet-Treat Burritos for Kids

Fry a tortilla in butter, place chosen ingredients in the center like a hot dog, start rolling, fold the sides toward the center, finish rolling, and gobble it up!

Ooey-Gooey Burrito: peanut butter, honey, and Trail Crumbs (page 29)
Cinnamon Tortilla: butter, cinnamon, and sugar or honey
Jammy Burrito: cream cheese and jam

Snow Ice Cream

This is a delicious refresher—especially suited for ski-touring trips and sweet moments.

Fill a cup with fresh, clean snow. Pour over the snow: apple or orange juice concentrate (may be bought in small cans) *or* any berry concentrate (in small bottles) *or* maple syrup *or* honey syrup. Eat or drink.

Beverages

It is important to get plenty of liquids while on the trail, as the extra energy you're using, the climate, and the altitude change can cause dehydration. Mountain streams offer the best drink available–however, please read the precautions about water on page 4.

Herbal Tonic Teas

When this book first came out, there were almost no herbal tea bags available on the market. *Simple Foods* was one of the first to recommend combining herbs to make a tonic tea to suit your taste and needs. The mild yet supportive nature of herbal teas has made them household words—*chamomile* for relaxation and stomachaches, *peppermint* for summer teas, *green tea* for its antioxidant qualities.

Here are a few herbal tonic combinations that help tone the body. You can drink them anytime. Explore for yourself to find the tastes and effects you enjoy. In general, cover 1–2 teaspoons of herbs with 1 cup of boiling water and steep in a covered pot or cup for 5–10 minutes. Herbs will usually settle to the bottom. If not, you can strain them out.

Sunrise in the Sierra
rosemary
hibiscus
rose hips
licorice root

Tea on the Trail 1
lemon verbena
chamomile
peppermint

Tea on the Trail 2
red clover
nettle
lemongrass
green oats
red raspberry

Artist's Vision Tea
green tea
chamomile
rose petals
spearmint

Owens River Tea
peppermint
alfalfa
red clover

Passion Plus 1
rosebuds
orange blossoms
lemongrass
red clover
nettle leaves

Passion Plus 2
grated gingerroot

Gentle Reflection Tea
catnip leaves
peppermint
lemon balm (a lemon-scented herb)
chamomile

Sunset in the Sierra
skullcap
passion flower
spearmint
lemongrass

Maté Latte

Yerba maté comes from a tree that is grown and culti-
vated in Paraguay. It is known to have 24 vitamins
and minerals, 15 amino acids, potent antioxidants,
and natural caffeine. Maté Latte is a wonderful early-
morning drink.

Use 1 heaping tablespoon yerba maté leaves per
cup of water. Place the yerba maté in a plastic single-
cup coffeemaker with filter paper. Set on top of cup,
moisten the yerba maté slightly with cool water, then
pour 1 cup hot (not boiling) water over it and let it
drain through.

For each serving, combine 1 cup tea with 2 tablespoons honey or maple syrup and ½ cup warm milk
(made with instant milk powder), and stir. Dust top
with cinnamon or cocoa powder.

Sun-Infused Herbal Tea

=============================

makes 1 quart

Early in the morning, as soon as you feel the sun beginning to warm your body, collect 4 cups of fresh purified water in a plastic quart bottle with a lid. Add 4 teaspoons dried herbs (see Herbal Tonic Teas, page 240) and set the bottle in the sun on a rock. Let it sit until the sun starts to go down, then strain and serve. You might want to put the bottle in a creek to cool it before straining.

Sun-Infused Herbal Lemonade

=============================

makes 1 quart

This is a sunshine-sweet drink, a luxury for the children who might be accompanying you on your journey. Follow directions for Sun-Infused Herbal Tea, above, except add 4 tablespoons of lemon juice and 2 tablespoons of honey when you add the herbs. Especially good for children are peppermint, chamomile, catnip, alfalfa, hyssop, and comfrey. These may be used individually or in combinations of two or three.

Ginger Tea

makes 1 cup

Ginger tea is a great calmative for the stomach.

½ teaspoon grated gingerroot
1 teaspoon honey

The ginger may be grated fresh in camp or grated at home and mixed with honey. Keep refrigerated until you pack up. Add *1 cup* boiling water and steep 10–15 minutes.

Rose Hip Elixir

makes 3 cups

This is very good on a cold winter night or early in the morning when your tent is still frost covered. It's high in vitamin C.

2 tablespoons rose hip powder
¼ cup maple syrup (also available powdered)
3 cups water

Combine rose hip powder and maple syrup, add *3 cups* hot water, and steep for 3–5 minutes.

Lemonade

makes 1 cup

Lemons are the best thirst quenchers. Take a few lemons for lemonade. One lemon sliced and added to a gallon of water will keep the water fresh if you have to carry it for several days.

2 tablespoons lemon juice
2 teaspoons honey

Combine lemon juice and honey and add *1 cup* water. You may have to use ¼ *cup* of hot water first, to dissolve the honey, and then add ¾ *cup* cold. For hot days, prepare the lemonade in the morning, put in a lidded plastic bottle, and place securely in a stream. In cold weather this drink is very good heated.

Lemon or Lime Water

This is very refreshing, and it feels good in your mouth.

Squeeze half a lemon or lime into your cup, and fill the cup with cold water. Swish it around and drink.

Horchata

━━━━━━━━━━━━━━━━━━━━━━━━━━━━

makes 4 cups

This is a nutritious Latin American drink. Serve it iced or hot.

1½ cups pumpkin seeds
⅔ cup almonds
4 tablespoons cinnamon
1 cup brown rice flour
1½ cups milk powder

At Home: Grind seeds and almonds in a blender or coffee grinder. In a frying pan, roast cinnamon over moderate heat, stirring constantly, until the aroma changes. Cool. Combine ingredients in a ziplock plastic bag.

In Camp: For cold Horchata, place 1 cup Horchata mixture in a container, and slowly stir in *4 cups* of cold water. Let stand 1 hour, covered. Shake or mix well and serve. Strain if desired. Sweeten with honey or maple syrup. For hot Horchata, place 1 cup Horchata mixture in your cook pot, and slowly stir in *4 cups* of water. Bring to a boil over moderate heat, stirring constantly. Cook about 1 minute, or until mixture thickens. Strain if desired, and serve. Sweeten with honey or maple syrup.

Variations: Add ½ cup cocoa to the dry mixture, roasting the cocoa with the cinnamon; add 1 teaspoon freshly ground allspice to the dry mixture.

Chocolate Almond Milk

makes 2 cups

Enjoy this rich-flavored, mild treat.

4 tablespoons almond meal, ground fine
2 heaping tablespoons cocoa
1 teaspoon vanilla
2 tablespoons honey
pinch of cardamom

At Home: Combine ingredients in a plastic ziplock bag.

In Camp: Pour contents of bag into a small cook pot. Add *2 cups* of boiling water, stir, pour into individual cups, and enjoy.

Hot "Chocolat"

makes 2 cups

This drink is hot, rich, and luscious.

6 tablespoons cocoa powder
6 tablespoons milk powder
1/8 teaspoon cloves
1/8 teaspoon chili powder
1/4 teaspoon cinnamon
1/4 teaspoon anise seeds *or* a few drops of anise extract
1/4 teaspoon vanilla

At Home: Combine ingredients in a ziplock bag.

In Camp: Pour contents of bag into a small cook pot. Pour *2 cups* of boiling water over all ingredients. Stir well and pour into individual cups.

Anise Milk Drink

The delicate flavor of anise makes this sweet drink a favorite.

1¼ cups milk powder
1 teaspoon anise seeds
2 tablespoons honey
butter, for hot drink

Make this on a day when you are going on a day hike away from camp and know you will want a good drink when you return. In a plastic quart bottle, combine milk powder, anise, and honey in *2–3 cups* of water. Cover and shake well. Set the bottle on a rock where the sun will hit it all day. When you return to camp in the evening, fill the rest of the bottle full of water and shake. If it is still too warm, place the bottle in a stream to cool. Strain and serve.

For a hot drink: Combine milk powder, honey, and anise with *4 cups* of water in your cook pot. Stir well and heat through until quite warm, but do not boil. Remove from heat, cover, and let stand for 5 minutes. Strain into cups and add a lump of butter in each cup. Children love it!

Carob Milk

This milk drink is a healthy replacement for chocolate milk. It's high in calcium and food energy.

1 cup milk powder
⅓ cup carob powder
1 tablespoon honey (optional)
½ teaspoon vanilla

Put *3 cups* of water in a plastic quart bottle. Add milk powder and carob. Cover tightly and shake well to mix. Stir honey in a small container or cup with a little bit of warm water to dissolve it. Add honey and vanilla to the quart bottle, and fill it almost to the top with water. Shake again, and serve.

For a hot drink: Combine all ingredients with *4 cups* of water in a cook pot. Heat through, stirring frequently, but do not boil.

Variation: Add 1 teaspoon of dry malt powder.

Cashew Milk

Pour this delicious milk over hot cereal or pudding, millet and dates, or rice and raisins. It's also a refreshing drink for small children.

1 cup raw cashews
1 tablespoon honey
1 teaspoon vanilla

At Home: Finely grind cashews in a blender, coffee grinder, or food mill, and mix in the honey and vanilla. Carry in a plastic bottle.

In Camp: Slowly add 2 *cups* of water and mix well.

Variation: For almond milk, follow recipe but blanch and peel the almonds first.

I picked my way

Through a mountain road,

And I was greeted

By a smiling violet.

—Bashō

4

Simple Remedies

Finding yourself along the trail with an unexpected ache or pain can be unpleasant. Quite often, however, a specific herb or food will soothe these minor ailments or injuries. Taking good care of yourself with nature's own remedies helps to keep you in balance.

Commonsense Advice

The recipes in this book are geared toward natural foods that help protect and restore the body and mind in a gentle way. This section describes a few simple natural remedies that can be used to help treat some common aches or pains you may encounter on the trail. These remedies are taken internally in the form of a tea or a pellet, or topically in the form of a gel, cream, poultice, or compress.

This section is meant not to replace any standard first aid or medical manual (see Books & Web Sites, page 272, for some good ones), but rather to calm, soothe, and perhaps prevent discomforts or minor ailments. Use common sense. In the mountains, if the problem or situation looks serious, go to a lower elevation as soon as possible and seek professional medical attention. If you are taking prescription medication or if you are pregnant, consult with your pharmacist before taking any herbal remedies.

To help keep yourself healthy from the moment you leave the trailhead, follow these tips: Drink lots of water; the average person should drink up to 4 quarts of fluid throughout the day. Use sunscreen, wear a hat, and remember to take rest and snack breaks when necessary. Dress properly for the weather and stay dry. Stay active and keep a steady, sustainable pace. Keep yourself well, remember to breathe, and above all, take care.

A Natural First Aid Kit

Herbs and homeopathic oils and creams are light-weight, don't take up much room in your pack, and can easily be stored in recycled film containers, plastic pillboxes, or tiny bottles. The natural products included in the list below will serve as a basic first aid kit for simple remedies on the trail. To build your own personalized kit, check out some of the many natural remedy books with more detailed information. We recommend a few in the Books & Web Sites section (page 272). Be sure to label all containers and carry the kit in a small stuff sack or airtight plastic bag. When assembled, this kit weighs less than a pound.

Simple Remedies Essentials

If the product listed below is an essential oil, dilute 1–3 drops in a teaspoon of vegetable oil.

Aloe (gel): for burns, cuts, sunburns, poison oak, hives

Apis (pellets): for bee stings, bug bites

Arnica (30c pellets): a homeopathic formula for pain, shock, stress, or emotional distress associated with pain

Calendula (gel or cream): an herbal salve for athlete's foot, burns, chapped lips, cuts and scrapes (helps heal and relieves pain), skin infections, insect stings, rashes, splinters

Cayenne powder: for bruises, colds, cold weather, muscle pain

Chamomile blossoms (dried): for indigestion, eye burn, muscle pain, restlessness or sleeplessness, splinters, sunburn

Citronella essential oil: for insect repellant

Cough drops (herbal), slippery-elm throat lozenges, or zinc: for colds, cough, sore throat

Fennel seeds: for cough, indigestion, insect stings, rest-lessness/sleeplessness, sore throat

Licorice root (dried): for colds and congestion, coughs, cold sores, constipation, fatigue

Rescue Remedy (cream): for bruises, bumps, irritated or damaged skin

Tea tree essential oil: for athlete's foot, insect bites, scratches, scrapes, stings

Vitamins B and C (tablets): for fatigue, stress, and healing (adds stamina and energy); vitamin C for colds

Vitamin E oil (capsules): for faster healing and reduction in scarring from cuts and scrapes, chapped lips, burns, sunburns

First Aid Essentials

Bandages (assorted sizes, including butterfly bandages)

Cloth or gauze pad for a compress or poultice

Cloth or paper tape

Cotton-tipped applicators

Disposable latex or vinyl gloves

Moleskin

Rolled gauze

Safety pins

Scissors

Sterile needle (for a blister)

Thermometer

Tweezers

Waterproof matches

Healing Foods

Some of the items you can use as remedies will not be in your first aid kit; they will already be in your pack among your food items. Ginger, honey, olive oil, rice, seaweed, vinegar, and oats are some of the nutritional items that will come in handy for specific needs. See Treating Common Hiking Ailments (page 258) for details.

Medicinal Teas

Medicinal teas can aid in treatment of some common ailments you may face on the trail. To make a medicinal tea using the flowers or leaves of the plant (an infusion), place 1–2 teaspoons of herb (see Treating Common Hiking Ailments, page 258, for specific recommendations) in a cup and pour 1 cup of boiling water over them. Let steep for 15–20 minutes. To decoct using the stems, roots, or bark, put 1–2 teaspoons in a pot, add 1 cup of water, cover, and simmer for 10–15 minutes. Strain, relax, and enjoy.

Poultices & Compresses

Poultices are used to speed up healing of muscle injuries or wounds. To make a poultice, use either fresh or dried herbs (see Treating Common Hiking Ailments, page 258, for specific recommendations), whole or ground. Wash the affected area and apply either fresh chopped herbs, boiled for 2–5 minutes, or dried herbs, boiled 5–10 minutes. If the dried herbs are powdery, mix with enough water to make a paste. If the herbs were boiled, squeeze out the water. Apply a little olive oil or vitamin E oil to the skin, then gently place the herbs over the affected area and cover with a clean cloth or gauze pad. Secure with rolled gauze strips. Replace every couple of hours.

To make a compress, brew a strong tea (called an herbal extract) of 1 tablespoon herbs to 1 cup water and pour into a bowl. Soak a soft cotton cloth or gauze pad in the extract, squeeze, and apply to the affected area. Repeat as the cloth cools or dries out.

Treating Common Hiking Ailments

Altitude Sickness. Climbing too high too fast can cause altitude sickness. The first symptoms are headache, loss of appetite, nausea (perhaps vomiting), sleeplessness, psychological weariness, unusual fatigue, and shortness of breath. To avoid this, you must take your time going up mountains, to acclimate. Climbers who mix rest periods with light exercise seem to acclimate faster than climbers who only rest. The amount of time it takes an individual to acclimate varies, and adequate hydration and nutrition are critical for everyone. If you experience the symptoms of altitude sickness, stop and rest. If the symptoms don't decrease within 48 hours, descend immediately.

Athlete's Foot. Athlete's foot is not caused by a few days' worth of hiking, but the condition may worsen while you're on the trail. If you suffer from athlete's foot, air out your feet often and apply calendula cream or tea tree essential oil before bedtime.

Blisters. The easiest way to prevent blisters is to make sure your shoes fit. As soon as you feel a blister coming on, stop and take care of it. Cut a donut shape from a piece of moleskin about ½ inch bigger than the blister and apply immediately. If the blister is larger than one inch across, wash the area with soap and water, and use a sterile needle to puncture the blister at the edge. Then gently press the liquid toward the hole you made, keeping the loose skin in place. Cover with a donut-shaped piece of moleskin and a clean sock. Change the moleskin once a day, removing it at night to air out the blister. To expedite healing, apply vitamin E oil on the second day. In the evening, use a poultice of chamomile. Keep your feet clean and dry.

Bruises. Apply cool wet cloths and press lightly until the pain subsides. Elevate the bruised area if possible. If the bruise still hurts after 48 hours, make a warm poultice of chamomile or cayenne and place it directly on the bruise. Cover the poultice (with your hand, another cloth, or a piece of plastic bag) and let it sit on the bruise for 5 minutes or so. Remove, apply a fresh poultice, and cover with a clean dressing. Leave both on overnight. Repeat if necessary. Massage in Rescue Remedy cream the following day.

Burns (minor). A burn is an open wound, and it should be treated as such. Immediately pour cool water over it, or immerse the area in cool water for 10–30 minutes, until the pain stops. Wash out any dirt by pouring soap and water or a saltwater solution (1 teaspoon salt to 1 cup of cold water) over the burn. Carefully pat dry and air briefly. Unless the area blisters or comes in contact with your clothing, do not cover the wound. If the area does blister, gently pour water over it, followed by some liquid soap and more water until the soap is rinsed completely off. Then cover with a nonstick gauze pad and tape it well away from the burned area. Avoid irritating the burn as much as possible. After 2 or 3 days you may apply aloe gel, calendula cream, or vitamin E oil. Keep the dressing clean and avoid touching the area with your bare hands. Replace with a clean dressing every day. As the burn dries, a gentle wash of chamomile tea is comforting.

Cold, cough, and sore throat. A cold comes on with sneezing and a runny nose (clear). If that starts on the trail, try to rest often and drink a lot of water. Take vitamin C and drink a hot cup of chamomile tea made with lemon and honey. Eat garlic and onions as much as you can (try Garlic Broth, page 119). For a decongestant tea, try licorice root. Sometimes a warm compress to the face helps open the sinuses. For coughing associated with a cold, take herbal cough drops or slippery-elm lozenges. Fennel, licorice root, or chamomile tea calms a cough. For a sore throat associated with a cold, dissolve 1 teaspoon salt in a cup of warm water and gargle, or gargle with a tea made from oregano or thyme. Fennel and licorice root tea is also very soothing to the throat. Or slowly dissolve slippery elm throat lozenges in your mouth, holding them toward the back of the throat.

If you get a high fever (over 101 degrees), or a fever doesn't go away in 24 hours, you should return and seek medical assistance. If any symptoms worsen (severe shortness of breath, sore throat, or coughing up phlegm that has color to it), seek medical attention.

Cold sores or canker sores (from too much sun). If you are susceptible to cold or canker sores, remember to use sun protection (sunscreen and a hat) and check the homeopathic counter for a product that suits your personal needs. Tea tree essential oil is helpful applied topically, and a tea of licorice root will support healing.

Cold weather. Plan ahead. Even in summertime, temperatures can drop radically at the end of the day in some hiking areas, especially at higher elevations. Wear layers of wool or microfiber shirts and sweaters, which will keep you warm even when wet. To prevent getting chilled, begin taking off layers as soon as you start to perspire. If you stop to rest, start putting the layers back on, slowly, to retain the body heat that you've built up from working. Most heat escapes through your head, so be sure to wear a warm hat.

If you do get cold and have trouble warming up, seek shelter, put on dry clothing, and wrap yourself in your sleeping bag. Pour heated water in your water bottle and hold it on the sides of the torso and in the groin area. Conserve energy, but keep muscles moving by making faces and repeatedly gripping with your fingers and toes. Drink warm sweetened teas, particularly ginger or cayenne, which will help you warm up. Garlic Broth (page 119) is a particularly helpful soup, and Toasted Oatmeal (page 103) calms and satisfies.

Hypothermia occurs when your body loses heat faster than it can produce it. Warning signs include slurred speech, headache, abdominal pains, stiff muscles, stumbling, irrational or confused activity (the individual may seem intoxicated), sudden bursts of energy followed by fatigue, and a loss of consciousness. If you or your fellow hikers experience these symptoms, seek medical help immediately.

Constipation. Constipation, often caused by not drinking enough water, may cause headaches and make you feel miserable. To prevent and soothe constipation, drink lots of water and eat oat bran, whole grain cereals, nuts, seeds, figs, prunes, raisins, apricots, applesauce, or blackberries. Massage your stomach by moving your right hand in a clockwise direction, pressing firmly, or moving your left hand from just under the rib cage down to the hip, also pressing firmly. Other remedies include swallowing a teaspoon of olive oil or drinking a tea with slippery elm powder, licorice root, or chamomile.

Cuts and scrapes (minor skin surface abrasion). If the bleeding is excessive or if there are any signs of complications, get to a doctor immediately. If the cut or scrape is minor, gently wash the area with soap and water and rinse with clear water, using disposable gloves if there is blood. For a small cut or scrape, allow a little blood to come out to clean the wound. Cover afflicted area with a sterile dressing and apply light pressure. Calendula cream, aloe gel, or a cool poultice of chamomile may be applied. After 2–3 days you may apply vitamin E oil or a rinse made with tea tree essential oil.

Diarrhea. Drink a tea of chamomile, rosemary, or oats. To rehydrate, eat rice gruel or grated carrot soup.

Emotional distress (associated with pain). Emotional distress that results from physical trauma such as a cut or a burn can actually exacerbate the feeling of pain. For these cases—to minimize the effects of shock, falls, bruising, burns, bleeding, bumps, or muscle pain—take 30c arnica pellets, as indicated on package.

Eye burn from glare, snow and/or sun. Snowblindness is the most common form of eye burn, which will feel like you have sand in your eyes. To prevent this, wear sunglasses that block UV light. To soothe the burn, make a tea of chamomile and soak a cloth in the tea when it's cool. Put the wet cloth over your closed eyes, allowing a few drops in to rinse your eyes. Soak for 5 minutes and repeat three times.

Fatigue or stress. As exhilarating as it is, backpacking is also quite exhausting. Try to pace your rest times throughout the day, and don't overexert yourself. If you are in a group, pace yourself with the children, the elderly, or with people who are not as fit as you are. Drink a lot of water and consider making a "sports drink" of ½ teaspoon salt, 1 teaspoon sugar or honey, and lemon in 4 cups of water. To replenish your system, get plenty of rest and drink licorice root, cayenne, peppermint, or green tea, or take vitamin B or vitamin C. Breathe freely, don't overeat, and keep your bowels loose.

Headache. Headaches can result from a variety of factors, but the most common cause in the backcountry is dehydration. If you think this is the case, slowly start drinking a quart of water. If you think the problem stems from hot weather, eye burn, constipation, emotional distress, or fatigue, follow remedies for those particular ailments. A headache that doesn't go away may signal a more serious medical problem; seek medical help as soon as possible.

Hot weather.   The best antidote for hot weather is water. You can also make a sports drink (see listing for Fatigue or stress). Wear lightweight, breathable clothing and a light-colored, wide-brimmed hat. For an exhilarating treat, dip the top of your head in a stream and let the cool water run down your face when you stand up. Or soak a bandana in a stream and loosely wrap it around your neck. Rinsing your hands and arms in water or soaking your feet for a few minutes will help, too. Drink a cool herb tea made with chamomile. Make a cool compress of green tea for prickly heat rash.

Indigestion or upset stomach.   For minor indigestion, try teas made with ginger, chamomile, or fennel. Take along some crystallized ginger to have after a heavy dinner as a treat.

Infections (minor topical).   If a minor wound gets slightly infected, carefully rinse the area with diluted tea tree essential oil (diluted with 1–3 drops per teaspoon vegetable oil) or with a calendula tea wash, or apply calendula gel. You may need to seek medical attention if the pain, swelling, redness, or tenderness increases; if there is a discharge of pus; if you get a fever; or if heat or red streaks extend away from the cut.

Insect stings.   To keep mosquitoes and other pests away, apply diluted citronella essential oil or diluted tea tree essential oil (1–3 drops per teaspoon of vegetable oil) to pulse points (wrists, behind ears, behind knees) and wear loose clothing that is tight around the ankles and wrists. For nonpoisonous stings, take two to three tablets of Apis one to three times per day; it alleviates hot, red, swollen, burning pain. Other remedies include applying calendula cream, lemon juice, vinegar, or diluted tea tree essential oil to the sting. You may also apply a fresh slice of onion or a wet black-tea bag to the sting. A cool fennel compress will reduce swelling. If you suspect that you were bitten by a poisonous insect, or if you have an allergic reaction to a bite or sting, seek medical help immediately.

Muscle pain.　Sore muscles go with the territory, so to speak, so be sure you have good support in your hiking boots, and avoid carrying a pack that is too heavy for your size and physical condition (a general rule is that the pack should be no more than 30 to 40 percent of your weight).

A great exercise to do when you take your pack off is to lie flat on your back, raise your knees high with your feet flat on the ground, and slightly lift your head so that the small of the back is pressed into the ground. This movement stretches the spine and counteracts the pressure of the day's hike.

For other muscle aches, rubs or compresses may be used on the painful area (but not on broken skin). Cool compresses of cloth soaked in strong chamomile tea are also soothing. Warm compresses may be made with cayenne powder in olive oil. (Generally, cool compresses are better for swelling and inflammation; warm compresses are better if there is no swelling.)

Remember that a charley horse is a muscle spasm caused by muscle contractions, which you can ease by stretching and moving the muscle. The pain and soreness will worsen if you stop using the muscle altogether. Also apply a warm chamomile compress, resoaking the cloth every 15 minutes or so.

Restlessness or sleeplessness.　Calm yourself down by focusing on your breathing and noticing your surroundings. Make sure you have on the proper clothes, that you eat well, and that you drink plenty of water. To relax, find a quiet moment and a nice spot to enjoy peace of mind and sip a calming tea of chamomile, fennel, or one of the Herbal Tonic Teas on page 240, such as Gentle Reflection Tea or Sunset in the Sierra.

Splinters. Wash the area of the splinter, and try to remove it with tweezers or your fingers. If the splinter is stubborn, apply calendula cream and cover with a bandage overnight or use a chamomile poultice. An old-fashioned remedy is to put a soft piece of soap (or dish soap) on the wound and cover with a damp bandage over night. Once you have removed the splinter, wash again and treat as a wound.

Sunburn, windburn, chapped skin. The air is thinner at higher altitudes, making it easier to get sunburned. To prevent sunburn and windburn or chapped skin, exercise caution in the elements and be sure to wear sun protection, a hat, and appropriate clothing. If you do get burned or chapped, immediately apply aloe gel to the damaged area. A cool wash made with chamomile is soothing. In the case of sunburn, swim in cold water or apply a cold wet cloth. Vitamin E oil or calendula cream are very effective if applied directly to chapped lips. After a burn, stay in the shade and repeat cold water applications as needed.

With all that evolving spread out behind us

We dance this frost fall morning away

On the sunward sides

Of granite boulders

—Doug Robinson

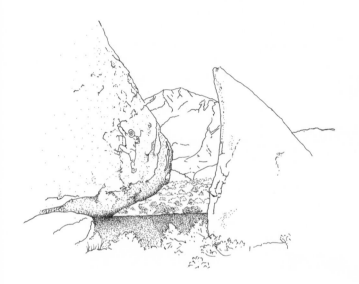

Food Sources

All of the foods we used can be found in your local grocery and health food stores or in ethnic grocery stores. Many of the food products we used in these recipes can be ordered online.

Amore
800-796-0116
Distributed by La Cucina Rustica, LP
P.O. Box 115, Wayne, IL 60184-0115
cybercucina.com
Manufacturers of small tubes of pastes, such as pesto, anchovy, sun-dried tomato, etc. Great additions to the pack to put on pasta or add in recipes.

Ancient Harvest Quinoa Corporation
310-217-8125
P.O. Box 279, Gardena, CA 90248
Organic quinoa distributor.

Barry Farm Enterprises
419-228-4640
20086 Mudsock Road, Wapakoneta, OH 45895
barryfarm.com
Organic dried vegetable and fruit products.

Eden Foods, Inc.
800-248-0320
701 Tecumseh Road, Clinton, MI 49236
edenfoods.com
Great dried mushrooms, snacks, noodles, and some dried fruit.

Fantastic Foods
800-288-1089
580 Gateway Drive, Napa, CA 94558
fantasticfoods.com
Mostly organic, delicious, lightweight prepackaged soups and one-pot meals centered around grains.

Gibbs Wild Rice
800-344-6378
P.O. Box 277, Deer River, MN 56636
gibbswildrice.com
Source for instant wild rice.

Guayaki Sustainable Rainforest Products
888-482-9254
P.O. Box 14730, San Luis Obispo, CA 93406
guayaki.com
Source for organic yerba maté.

The Just Tomatoes Company
800-537-1985
P.O. Box 807, Westley, CA 95387
justtomatoes.com
Dehydrated and freeze-dried vegetables and fruits. Vine- or tree-ripened, handpicked at peak conditions. Washed, cut, and dried in dehydrators at low temperatures to preserve color, flavor, and nutrients. An excellent source of nutritious foods.

Mendocino Sea Vegetable Company
707-895-2996
P.O. Box 455, Philo, CA 95466
mendocinoseavegetablecompany.com
A complete line of hand-harvested sea vegetables. May be bought in bulk. Good reputation for products of high-quality appearance, taste, and purity.

More Than Gourmet, Inc.

800-860-9385
929 Home Avenue, Akron, OH 44310
morethangourmet.com
Gourmet stocks to be used as broth or in sauces. Excels in Old World sauces and stocks that have no chemicals, preservatives, or MSG; they require no refrigeration, and the condensed stock packages weigh 1.5 ounces (making approximately 8½ cups of broth). Great classic French flavor.

Old River Fruits

Neufeld Farms
707-975-4605
P.O. Box 4405, Petaluma, CA 94955
oldriverfruits.com
Incredible dried fruits. Obscure varieties. Bing cherries; Betty Ann, Kelsy, and Friar plums; September Sun peaches; Ruby apricots; more than six varieties of pluots (a cross between a plum and an apricot), and much more. Fruits are not sprayed, and only natural fertilizers are used. Sold at many farmers' markets. Delicious.

Rising Tide Sea Vegetables

707-964-5663
P.O. Box 1914, Mendocino, CA 95460
risingtide@mcn.org or www.loveseaweed.com
Hand-harvested sea vegetables that have no natural salts or sugars on their surface. Packaged airtight in double or triple bags.

Salmon Etc.

800-354-7256
P.O. Box 6594, Ketchikan, AK 99901
salmonetc.com
Natural salmon products, including wild Alaska smoked salmon and salmon jerky. No MSG.

The Spice House
312-274-0378
1941 Central Street, Evanston, IL 60201
thespicehouse.com
Good source of tomato powder.

SunOrganic Farm
888-269-9888
411 S. Las Posas Road, San Marcos, CA 92069
sunorganicfarm.com
Great source for bulk organic nuts, grains, beans, dried fruits and vegetables, snacks, and nut butter.

Vital Choice Seafood
800-608-4825
605 30th Street, Anacortes, WA 98221
vitalchoice.com
Canned wild red Nass River sockeye salmon. Can be ordered by the case online. Also sells wild organic blueberries.

Whole Spice
415-472-1750
292 North San Pedro Road, Suite B
San Rafael, CA 94903
Wide variety of high-quality spices (some organic).

Books & Web Sites

Books

Bond, Marybeth. *Gutsy Mamas: Travel Tips and Wisdom for Mothers on the Road.* Sebastopol, CA: Travelers' Tales, 1997 (c/o O'Reilly & Associates, Inc., 101 Morris Street, Sebastopol, CA 95472).

Bove, Mary, N.D. *An Encyclopedia of Natural Healing for Children and Infants.* New Canaan, CT: Keats Publishing, 2001.

Carline, Jan D., Ph.D., Martha J. Lentz, R.N., Ph.D., and Steven C. Macdonald, M.P.H., Ph.D. *Mountaineering First Aid: A Guide to Accident Response and First Aid Care.* Seattle: The Mountaineers, 1972 (1001 SW Klickitat Way, Suite 201, Seattle, WA 98134).

El Molino Mills. *El Molino Best Recipes.* Alhambra, CA: Self-published, 1953.

Food Standards Agency. *McCance and Widdowson's: The Composition of Foods.* 6th summary ed. London: Institute of Food Research, Royal Society of Chemistry, 2002.

Gusman, Jill. *Vegetables from the Sea: Everyday Cooking with Sea Greens.* New York: HarperCollins Publishers, 2003.

Hart, John. *Walking Softly in the Wilderness.* 3rd ed. San Francisco: Sierra Club Books, 1998.

Hurd, Rosalie, and Frank Hurd. *Ten Talents.* Chisholm, MN: Self-published, 2003 (Box 86A, Route 1, Chisholm, MN 55719).

Isaac, Jeffrey, P.A.-C. *The Outward Bound Wilderness First Aid Book.* New York: The Lyon's Press, 1998.

Lewallen, Eleanor, and John Lewallen. *Sea Vegetable Gourmet Cookbook.* Mendocino, CA: Mendocino Sea Vegetable Company, 1996 (P.O. Box 1265, Mendocino, CA 95460).

Lockie, Andrew. *The Family Guide to Homeopathy.* New York: Simon and Schuster, 1993.

Nearing, Helen. *Simple Food for the Good Life.* White River Junction, VT: Chelsea Green Publishing Company, 1999.

Ody, Penelope. *The Complete Medicinal Herbal.* New York: D. K. Publishing, 1993.

The Ohsawa Foundation, Inc. *Zen Cookery.* Los Angeles: Ignoramus Press, 1985.

Pallasdowney, Rhonda. *The Complete Book of Flower Essences.* Novato, CA: New World Library, 2002.

Panos, Maesimund B., M.D., and James Heimlich. *Homeopathic Medicine at Home: Natural Remedies for Everyday Ailments and Minor Injuries.* New York: Penguin Putnam, 1981.

Robinson, Doug. *A Night on the Ground, a Day in the Open.* La Crescenta, CA: Mountain N'Air Books, 1996. (P.O. Box 12540, La Crescenta, CA 91224).

Tilton, Buck, M.S., and Tom Burke, M.D. *The Wilderness First Responder: A Text for the Recognition, Treatment and Prevention of Wilderness Emergencies.* Guilford, CT: Globe Pequot Press, 1998 (available through wmi.com).

U.S. Department of Agriculture. *Handbook of the Nutritional Value of Foods in Common Units.* Mineola, NY: Dover Publications, 1975.

Web Sites

These are continually expanding and changing, but here are some we recommend:

backpackerspantry.com
Good place to find accessories for cook stoves: camp ovens, scorch buster, and Pot Parka, to name a few.

campmor.com
Wide range of camping and backpacking equipment. Good prices on backpacking tools.

GSI.com
Outdoor cookware and accessories. This is where you can get GSI products direct. They sell an 8-inch and a 10-inch skillet and two sizes of cook sets that we highly recommend, along with many other handy items.

herbalremedies.com
Offers a wide range of herbal products, including tinctures, teas, capsules, and more.

KarynSanders.com
Karyn Sanders is a clinical herbal practitioner and herbal educator. She hosts a radio program called *The Herbal Highway* on public radio (KPFA).

movingoverstone.com

Doug Robinson is the owner and lead guide at this climbing school and guide service for rock climbing, backcountry skiing, mountaineering, and corporate training in the San Francisco Bay Area and High Sierra.

nols.com

NOLS, the National Outdoor Leadership School, is the premier teacher of outdoor skills and leadership. It offers 10-day to full-semester courses in the world's most spectacular wilderness classrooms.

outwardbound.com

Outward Bound is a nonprofit educational organization offering wilderness programs for adults and teens. Courses last between 4 days and 12 weeks.

wmi.com

The Wilderness Medicine Institute provides the highest-quality education and information for the recognition, treatment, and prevention of wilderness emergencies.

Index

cashews *(continued)*
  Soup, 139; Rice Curry, 184; Trail Crumbs, 29. *See also* nuts
Cashew Sauce, 166
cayenne powder, 255, 259, 262
Celery Soup, Cream of, 137
Cereals, 96–104
chamomile blossoms: about, 255; in poultices, 258, 259, 262, 264; for sunburn, windburn, chapped skin, 265; in teas, 260, 261, 263
chapped skin remedies, 265
cheese: about, 7; Alpine Spaghetti, 188; Basic White Sauce, 159; Beer Fondue, 208; Burritos, 209; Carrot Cakes, 64; Cheese Cookies, 37; Cheese Sauce, 160; Chili, 176; Corn Bread, 112; Corn Cheese Dumplings, 148; Crab à la King, 217; Cream of Celery Soup, 137; Fresh Vegetable Soup, 86; Fruit & Noodle Salad, 194; Greens & Quick-Cooking Pasta or Quinoa, 92; Hot Pot Soup, 128; Macaroni & Cheese, 187; Mashed Potatoes & Greens, 90; Minestrone, 127; Miso Soup, 121; Mountain Gruel, 205; Nut Butter Soup, 139; One-Pot Grain & Seafood, 201; Polenta Cheese Stew, 195; Polenta Mush, 196–97; Potato Cheese Soup, 134; Potatoes & Mushrooms, 88; Presto Pasta, 189; Rye Batter Bread, 116; Salsa Soup with Corn Cheese Dumplings, 129; Skillet Bake, 87; Spinach Cheese Casserole, 186; Spinach Cheese Soup, 133; Spinach Clam Soup, 126; Stuffed Portobello, 89; Sun-Dried Tomato Pasta, 190; Sweet-Treat Burritos for Kids, 237; Swiss Fondue, 207; Taste of Santa Fe, 175; Walnut Cheese Burgers, 65

Cheese Cookies, 37
Cheese Sauce, 160
chia seeds: High-Protein Almond Cookies, 39; High-Protein Crackers, 50; Polenta Cakes, 62; Seed Cakes, 74; Seed Date Fudge, 45; Sesame Chia Crackers, 49. *See also* seeds
children, camping with, xi
Chili, 176
chilies, about, 10
Chili Sauce, 153
Chili Sauce, Red Barbecue, 162
chlorine water treatment, 5–6
chocolate: about, 7; Chocolate Almond Milk, 247; Chocolate Poppers, 41; Cup of Custard, 231; Hot "Chocolat," 247; Skillet Brownies, 226; Steamed Chocolate Fudge Pudding, 234–35. *See also* candy; carob
Chocolate Almond Milk, 247
Chocolate Poppers, 41
Cilantro Lime Dressing, 79
Cinnamon Orange Liquor Fudge, 46
citronella essential oil, 255, 263
Citrus Cream Cheese Spread, 78
Clam Chowder, 140
clams: Clam Chowder, 140; Clams over Pasta, 212; Marinara Sauce, 152; Spinach Clam Soup, 126
Clams over Pasta, 212
coconut: Apricot Date Fudge, 45; Anzacs, 38; Carob Fudge, 44; Chocolate Poppers, 41; Coconut Almond Barley Cakes, 73; Granola, 35; Hot Cracked Millet Cream Cereal, 101; Pecan Fudge, 43; Raw Granola (Muesli), 36; Rice Curry, 184; Sesame Animal Crackers, 53; Sesame Crisp Candy, 47; Sesame Seed Cookies, 40; Soaked Cereal, 98; Thai

Claudia Axcell is a former trail guide and professional baker. She lives in Bishop, California. **Vikki Kinmont Kath,** a resident of Sebastopol, California, is a photographer and professional cook. **Diana Cooke,** a graduate of the Cordon Bleu in London, makes her home in Bishop, California.

10/05

SEC